My Favourite Person

A Shining Star
Edited by Donna Samworth

First published in Great Britain in 2010 by:

Young Writers

Young Writers
Remus House
Coltsfoot Drive
Peterborough
PE2 9JX
Telephone: 01733 890066
Website: www.youngwriters.co.uk

All Rights Reserved
Book Design by Spencer Hart & Tim Christian
© Copyright Contributors 2009
SB ISBN 978-1-84924-704-7

Foreword

Our 'My Favourite Person 2009' poetry competition attracted young aspiring poets to show their admiration for those who have made an impact in their life. What better way to let those closest know how much they are appreciated.

We are delighted to present this thoughtful collection. After reading through the hundreds of entries it is clear the amount of enthusiasm and love that went into writing these poems, therefore we hope you'll agree they are an inspiring and heart-warming read.

Young Writers was established in 1991 to promote poetry and creative writing to schoolchildren and encourage them to read, write and enjoy it. Here at Young Writers we are sure you'll agree that this special edition achieves our aim and celebrates today's wealth of young writing talent. We hope you enjoy this anthology for many years to come.

Contents

Vickie O'Sullivan (11) 1	Martha Okon (12) 26
Charlotte Begley (12) 2	Matteo Sarro (11) 26
Ariam Semere (10) 3	Aasia Majid (10) 27
Ferdus Akther (12) 4	Rebecca Whiting (12) 27
Megan McKee (10) 5	Dominic Starkey (11) 28
Emily Smith (12) 6	Bobbie Smith (11) 28
Annabel Smith (12) 7	Rosie Margolis (12) 29
Temitope Odunubi (11) 8	Angie Choudhury (9) 29
Scarlett Secrett (11) 9	Heather Jeffrey (11) 30
Katie Thow (11) 10	Lucy Card (9) 30
Maria Van Hoof (10) 10	Anna Nelson (10) 31
Ehmna Aslam (11) 11	Hope Newman (11) 31
Kara Wright (11) 11	Beth Robinson (10) 32
Kayleigh Hopcroft (11) 12	Callum O'Reilly (10) 32
Saoirse Yardley (11) 12	Alex Wood (9) 33
Kalsey Herian (10) 13	Ben Finn (11) 33
April John (10) 13	Sophie Glandfield (10) 34
Matthew Wilson (11) 14	Ben Pearce (10) 34
Elleanor Rearie (9) 14	Pessi Frankel (11) 35
Sabir Assad Amin (10) 15	Lauren Grace Gallacher (9) 35
Natasha Medcalf (6) 15	Amber Madden (10) 36
Abigail Harris (11) 16	Ruby Haggie 36
Serena Piacentini (9) 16	Megan Phoenix (12) 37
Jessica Foskett (15) 17	Kerri-Ann Middleton (11) 37
Kelvin Ihama (9) 17	Somto Egboga (11) 38
Ee Von Foo (9) 18	Katelyn John (6) 38
Zenani Johnson (12) 18	Anisah Bulsari (11) 39
Sally Lancaster (10) 19	Sasha Moore (10) 39
Verity Fretwell (11) 19	Rosie Scott (10) 40
Emma Reeves (11) 20	Philip Vergis Mathew (10) 41
Lathan Mahalingam (11) 20	Megan Jones (11) 42
Phoebean Olanrewaju (10) 21	Jonathan Baker (10) 42
Fola Taiwo (10) 21	Maddy Baker (10) 43
Chloe Nicklin (11) 22	Amber Throop (10) 43
Lois Type (10) 22	Rebecca Turnbull (12) 44
Sumayyah Iqbal (10) 23	Scarlet Larby (9) 44
Toby Maitland (11) 23	Maqdus Iqbal (9) 45
Emily Baldwin (11) 24	Christy Duvenhage (11) 45
Lucy MacKenzie (8) 24	Ben Gregoriou (11) 46
Lillie-Mai Reilly (11) 25	Yolanda Quartey (9) 46
Jodie Smith (10) 25	Alexandria Allan-Sutcliffe (8) 47

Sebastian Zahn (10)	47	Lorelei Makepeace Nielsen (11)	70
Georgia Franks (10)	48	James Burnham (9)	70
Dayo Nylander (11)	48	Rachael Forsythe (10)	71
Chloe Verebelyi (10)	49	Charlie Mills (10)	71
Kiara Knight (9)	49	Layla Moghaddam (10)	72
Charlotte Selby (11)	50	Niamh Woods (8)	72
Sadie Colley (11)	50	Aisha Kayani (11)	73
Dayna Cook (11)	51	Emily-Jane Bayliss (10)	73
Kristina Werner (10)	51	Erin Seabrook (10)	74
Evie Bull (8)	52	Fiona Chaitezvi (11)	74
Kyle Wilkinson (12)	52	Zainah Muddassir (11)	75
Jaydene Reece-Gardner (11)	53	Samuel Howell (11)	75
Georgia O'Keeffe (11)	53	Adam Bell (9)	76
Muhmmed Fahed (10)	54	Fatimah Mohd-Fauzi (8)	76
Kelsey Burdell (12)	54	Marissa Patel (11)	77
India Howard (11)	55	David Swan (11)	77
Courtney Gaunt (11)	55	Shivani Nathu (12)	78
Sonia Bhangal (10)	56	Isobel Sword (10)	78
Nana Nkyidjour (10)	56	Osragli Elezi (11)	79
Ellie Harrison (11)	57	Esraa Fahmy (8)	79
Charlie Mitchell (10)	57	Holly Chambers (10)	80
Hannah Greenstreet (14)	58	Sophie Hall (10)	80
Ellie McGann (12)	58	Bethany Cook (11)	81
Jessica Finley (8)	59	Kirran Khan (12)	81
Meedia Abid (11)	59	Ellie Barnfield (10)	82
Anna Freire Camacho (11)	60	Niamh Lundy (11)	82
Elisha Stuckey (9)	60	Cassie Devereux (10)	83
Shams Sair (11)	61	Teerith Sehmi (12)	83
Leah Georgina Randall (11)	61	Ella Rayment (10)	84
Rachel Cunliffe (11)	62	Tyler Poyner (11)	84
Shannon Richardson (8)	62	Kain Hooper (11)	85
Samantha Griffin (11)	63	Annabel Streete (11)	85
Deanne Cope (10)	63	Georgia Woodley (11)	86
Jack Mapstone (10)	64	Charlotte Mills (11)	86
Alicia Price (10)	64	Olivia Barker (11)	87
Cameron Barkshire (10)	65	Emily McGowan (9)	87
Caitlin Jones (12)	65	Chloe Cox (10)	88
Faye Brightmore (10)	66	Sophie Woolnough (10)	88
Micheala Chan (12)	66	Eloise Hadley (10)	89
Monique Jose (11)	67	Jade Thompson (11)	89
Darcie Lonsdale (9)	67	Holly Young (11)	90
Safoorah Dhalech (10)	68	Mariyah Wolfenden (10)	90
Caitlin Doherty (8)	68	Ellie Kate Trafford (10)	91
Lucy Chandler (10)	69	Esther Darling (10)	91
Rebecca Webster (11)	69	Rebecca Andrew (10)	92

Muna Elayeh (11)	92
Sophie Cox (11)	93
Sohail Ahmed (11)	93
Ruby Gill (10)	94
Natasha Baugh (11)	94
Rhiannon Gilbey (9)	95
Prakriti Arora (7)	95
Keira Chew (10)	96
Storm Rose (10)	96
Eleanor Cunningham (10)	97
Kate Horwell (13)	97
Jordi Morgan (12)	98
Megan Delaney (11)	98
Maisy Syratt (8)	99
Charlie Hall (11)	99
Ellis Anderson (10)	100
Pia Joyce (8)	100
Alana Emms (11)	101
Leila Charteris (10)	101
Emily Wong (11)	102
Isla Hoad (11)	102
Emma Batchelor (10)	103
Chloe O'Hara (10)	103
Anna McKay (9)	104
Sasha Antoine (10)	104
Lakhraj Dhiman (11)	105
Daisy Ellis (10)	105
Waqas Arshad (11)	106
Will Bourn (10)	106
Bethany Halley (10)	107
Domantas Stankus (9)	107
Isra Dar (12)	108
Ethan Cleary (11)	108
Grace Robertson (9)	109
Conah Casson-Suratan (11)	109
Jade Palmer (9)	110
Samuel Vaughan (10)	110
Joe Lidgett (11)	111
Roisin McKeegan (11)	111
Shannon Windle (12)	112
Tasha Bull (11)	112
Emily Davies (11)	113
Cait Stead (11)	113
Nadine Barber (11)	114
Muna Abdelrahman (11)	114
Mia Critchley (11)	115
Asviny Arulanantham (9)	115
Asmaa Hafez (9)	116
Milly Tye (9)	116
Amelia Mapson (9)	117
Chloe Glover (11)	117
Emma Jane Langhorn (11)	118
Habibur Rahman (10)	118
Zoe Laxton (10)	119
Ceri-Ann Field (10)	119
Zainab Patel (11)	120
Isaac Lowry (10)	120
Eliza Wren (10)	121
Anna Fitzgeorge (11)	121
Beth Conroy (11)	122
Olivia Brewin (8)	122
Eve Patton (9)	123
Kurran Landa (10)	123
Willa Elliot (11)	124
Melanie Gunetilleke (11)	124
Amy Phillips (9)	125
Kristin Russell-Rickards (10)	125
Jemma Watson (11)	126
Olivia Alexander (10)	126
James Stuart Rennie (10)	127
Jack Rossiter (10)	127
Phoebe Collingridge (11)	128
Kareena Akhtar (5)	128
Zara Nicol (11)	129
Adele Harris (11)	129
Zanjeeb Butt (10)	130
Diveena Nanthakumaran (11)	130
Promise Emesi (9)	131
Georgina McCann (10)	131
Victor Salako (11)	132
Sarrah Boukheroufa (9)	132
Demi Coates (11)	133
Kiran Banerjee (8)	133
Rachel Ann Marsh (9)	134
Melissa Fear (9)	134
Lily-Rose Morris-Zumin (9)	135
Samuel Portwood (11)	135
Freya Seekings (10)	136
Naomi Nioku (10)	136
Louisa Sanderson (11)	137

Caitlin Collins (10)	137
Benjamin Juliff (5)	138
Chloe May (11)	138
Marco Cardoni (11)	139
Kirsty Brickles (11)	139
Millie Lépora (11)	140
Rachel Cullen (12)	140
Megan Campbell (12)	140
Macauley Hatley (10)	141
Callum Burkitt (10)	141
Ellie Bannister (10)	141
Callum Draycott (11)	142
Francesca Leftley (11)	142
Amy Davies (11)	143
Emily Owen (9)	143
Emily Lee (11)	144
Alicia Clarke (9)	144
Ebonie Barnes (11)	145
Kelly Oforiwaa (6)	145
Holly Gooding (11)	146
Billie Foster (10)	146
Lucy Osborne (9)	146
Emily Gibbs (10)	147
Amy Lewington (10)	147
Daniel Davies (10)	147
Sophie Lancelot (11)	148
Grace Benfield (9)	148
Jade Mall (9)	148
Aisha Dechicha (6)	149
Natasha Richardson (10)	149
Jennifer Shawulu Nggada (6)	149
Eleanor Lowe (9)	150
Joanna Sands (9)	150
Erin Lawlor (11)	150
Jazmin Lake (9)	151
Katelyn Reeves (9)	151
Robert Warden (10)	151
Rhiannon Thomas (6)	152
Connor Knill (11)	152
Lucy Geoghegan (11)	152
Olivia Sims (10)	153
Inthesar Ar-Rahman (9)	153
Ethan Good (10)	153
Chloe Human (10)	154
Hamish Wilson (11)	154
Lauren Ivy Walsh (9)	154
Orlagh McCloskey (10)	155
Lewis Kettlety (8)	155
Michael Wales (8)	155
Miranda Tossell Laszkiewicz (9)	156
Bryony Gooch (10)	156
Hollie Symmons (8)	156
Courtney Lewis (10)	157
Lucy Knight-Summers (11)	157
Ryan Munro (8)	157
Beth Alice Edmonds (11)	158
Fatima Noor (10)	158
Caitlin McMullan (9)	158
Brandon Carter (10)	159
Lewis Isaac (9)	159
Jessica Tennant (11)	159
Maddie Hardern (9)	160
Chloe Pitman (10)	160
Daniel Lock (9)	160
Jodie Passmore (11)	161
Sarah Edwards (11)	161
Godgift Emesi (11)	162

The Poems

My Favourite Person

My favourite person in the world is my mum.
We have had a special connection since I was in her tum.

One evening she was watching telly,
Eating ice cream and jelly,
She let out a din,
When she felt a pain from within,
She knew I was on the way,
And I was going to be born that day,

And she was right,
Because that night,
I came into the world.

We are always doing things together,
We are going to be close forever,
She is very special to me,
She is everything I want to be,
She is kind and caring,
Loving and sharing,
She is my best friend,
And when I am with her the fun never ends,

She is always there,
With love and care,
When I'm good, when I'm bad,
When I'm lonely, when I'm sad,
She's always ready, to listen to love,
She possesses a gift from high above,
The gift to be loved by all she knows,
And to be sorely missed if she goes,

When time comes and she needs care,
I'd like to think that I'd be there.

Vickie O'Sullivan (11)

When You Have A True Friend

The best thing in life
Is having a true friend.
Someone who stays beside you,
Until the very end.

Why race through life,
When there's no prize at the end?
Life is much better,
When you have a true friend.

True friends stick together,
Whatever they do.
And a quality they always share,
Is that they're always true.

Why race through life,
When there's no prize at the end?
Life is much better,
When you have a true friend.

A true friend is someone,
Who knows you better than yourself.
Someone who sees you every day,
In sickness or in health.

Why race through life,
When there's no prize at the end?
Life is much better,
When you have a true friend.

They'll show friendship in a present,
Maybe a hug or smile.
Or maybe they'll run to see you,
If you haven't seen them for a while.

Why race through life,
When there's no prize at the end?
Life is much better,
When you have a true friend.

True friends are not greedy,
Selfish or unkind.
If you have a true friend,
Then this is what you'll find.

Why race through life,
When there's no prize at the end?
Life is much better,
When you have a true friend.

Charlotte Begley (12)

My Parents

My mum and dad
Help me when I'm sad
They're friendly and kind
If you don't like them you are out of your mind
They care for me and make sure I'm fine
And I'm so glad these parents are mine
They help me with any problems at all
They play with me, skipping, tag and ball
They cook for me and give me food to eat
And buy clothes for me from my head to my feet
I love, love, love the treats they give
It is a lovely way to live
They take me to clubs and take me to school
They buy me clothes so I look cool
There is my number one mum
Who is lots of fun
Then there is my number one dad
Who I've got and I'm glad
My parents are funny, unique, one of a kind
They are a really amazing find
I'm so glad they are my parents!

Ariam Semere (10)

My Special Spark - My Mum

With this special person I feel utter bliss,
She's the one person I will always miss,
I'm so glad that in my life she does exist,
She's the only person I know with a warm-hearted kiss,
That's why Mum you are my shining ruby,
My special person, my bright spark!
Every difficulty we discuss we solve together,
That's why my mum will always be in my heart forever.
She is always the one who stands beside me in school life,
And that's why Mum you are my guide in everything you teach me in,
I really love my mum since her words are nothing compared to her love,
That is shared with me,
That's why Mum you are my special person, my star, my life!
She knows when to draw the line,
She knows when I feel sick or fine,
Without her I would feel declined,
She is none other than a mummy of mine,
That's why you are my diamond, my special person and my every breath!
You are my heart which pumps blood to my whole body,
Without you my heart and I can't live,
At the same second you are my brain,
Which directs me to the right road.
Without you my brain can't think
That's why Mum you are all mine,
My fairy tale wishes, three words Mum,
I love you!
Something which will always be true,
Your love for me is renewed,
One more time, I love you,
My one in a million person,
My grand finale,
My spark in life and my every breath is yours
You are my greatest gift in life!
Every day I embrace your love, forever and ever
And we will continue to do so together forever
And I'll hand you my hand as you hand me yours
We together will always be stars that are always bright,

As mother and daughter,
We all will *unite!*
Mother and daughter, love is incomparable
To any love shared in the world!

Ferdus Akther (12)

My Favourite Person - The Foot Doctor

She's the foot doctor
And she looks after feet
Her name is Jane
And she's very nice to meet
She made my verruca go away
It was probably round about last May!

She's the foot doctor
And she looks after feet
She works in Middleton
And she's very, very sweet
She made my verruca go away!
It was probably round about the 23rd May!

She's the foot doctor
And she looks after feet
Go in her surgery, it's never not neat
She made my verruca go away
Thank you Jane, I'll remember that day!

She's the foot doctor
And she looks after feet
When you're waiting for a check up
There's always a seat
She made my verruca go away
Thank you Jane, I don't know what to say
Thank you. Thank you. Thank you!

So if you ever need a foot doctor
Jane's the one to call
She'll have you right as rain
In no time at all!

Megan McKee (10)

Rexy The Dino

Here's my favourite person
I love him dearly
He is a half-deaf dinosaur
And can't hear very clearly

He is a T-rex called Rexy
He is my own sole creation
I keep him nice and warm and safe
In my imagination

I'm bored, I'll visit him
I say hello, and we embrace
Then we let go and I challenge him
To a lengthy, difficult race!

I came back to Earth with a 'plop'
(Literally, I slipped on the floor's lino)
And, I had to admit, even though he's made up,
I really missed my dino . . .

Last week, I was bored
So I saw him again
This time, we went abroad
We went to sunny Spain

Today, in the jungle, we saw weird bugs
Even an enormous praying mantis
Later, we decided to have an adventure
In the Lost City of Atlantis!

Now I'm seeing him tomorrow
After all, he is my best friend
And I know one thing for sure -
Our friendship will never end.

Emily Smith (12)

My Aunty Ails

My aunty Ails
She's such great fun
Telling us jokes
She never makes us glum.

My aunty Ails
She works in lots of schools
She's a psychologist
Now that has to be cool.

My aunty Ails
She's really kind
She's one of those people
Who are really hard to find.

My aunty Ails
She's a clumsy clot
Slipping over in weddings
And that's not the lot.

My aunty Ails
Her talent is to surf
She also loves to travel
Around the universe.

My aunty Ails
She's getting married quite soon
All the cousins are bridesmaids
And Rick is the groom.

My aunty Ails
She's as funny as a clown
Please, please stay this way
And always stay around.

Annabel Smith (12)

My Brother, Tariq

Tariq is 13, older than me, I am 11.
When he picks me up I feel like I'm flying in Heaven.
He's nearly 14 and big and strong,
People are always getting his age wrong.
You see he is so tall, broad, he looks older.
I'm small and petite, my brother can carry me on his shoulder.
He makes me laugh so hard I cry,
My brother's wit is very dry.
To me he is funny, I look up to him a lot.
For some strange reason, he always wears odd socks.
Now that is funny, he can be crazy and a little lazy,
That part drives Mum up the wall.
Tariq and I though, always manage to have a ball.
We play football and all kinds of games together,
I really hope we will be this close forever.
I love my brother, he's always there for me.
He is protective, yet allows me to be free.
Sometimes we argue and fight
But we always put things right.
Tariq is in Year 9 at Patcham High,
I'm in Year 7, just started, so far it's all right.
Tariq is the only one who makes me laugh like mad,
Even if I'm feeling a little sad.
He will carry me upstairs if I fall asleep,
Later, when he goes to bed, he has a little peep.
He's a bit of a softy, he says I look cute all snuggled up.
My big brother is *a star,*
I know he will go far.
He is clever, funny, has lots of friends.
Tariq will be like this till the very end.

Temitope Odunubi (11)

Ruby

Here's a little poem,
About a fabulous girl I know,
Her name is Ruby,
And every letter of her name stands for something,
Something special,
And this is how it goes,
R is for red,
Because that's what people call her,
And a ruby is red,
And they are very beautiful,
U means you,
Because she loves and cares,
Puts others before herself,
It's not just about me for her,
It's also you,
B is for beautiful,
Because that's what she is,
If you say she is not,
You're telling a lie,
And Y is for yellow,
Which is a colour I think she doesn't like,
But I think yellow is bright,
And she is very, very bright,
And that's my little poem,
About a fabulous girl I know,
She will always be the best sister,
That you could possibly think of,
There's no friend like a sister,
And no sister quite like you.

Scarlett Secrett (11)

Young Writers

My Mum!

My favourite person
Is my mum Donna Thow
She is kind, loving and gentle
But sometimes gives me a row.

She is always doing my washing
And she can't wait until I can do my own
I don't know what I'd do without her
I would not manage alone.

Tidying my room is boring
And she's always nagging me
One day it will be tidy
But she'll just have to wait and see.

But I would miss her shouting,
'Katie, tidy your room!'
But it will never be tidy
Well, not anytime soon.

Ignore what I've written above
This verse is the best
The love my mum gives me
Would pass any mum's test.

If there was a list of mums
My mum would be at the top
And if any more mums came to my doorstep
I would send away the lot!

Katie Thow (11)

My Cat

C ocoa is so cuddly
O thers think she's noisy
C ute and comical is her nickname
O pen the tuna and she'll come running
A lways on the lookout for intruders.

Maria Van Hoof (10)

Myrth

There's no one like her
She is the best
You can't beat her
She's better than the rest.

She is so funny
And so much fun
Can't be beaten
Can't be won.

We went to nursery
And part of school
Then she moved to Cornwall
That was not cool.

We sometimes speak
On MSN
We nearly met up
When we were 10.

Just last week
Yes, you've guessed
I went to Cornwall
It was the best.

We met up
It was so much fun
Me and my best friend
Shine like the sun!

Ehmna Aslam (11)

My Mum Is So Special

My mum is that shooting star that runs across the sky.
My mum is the blossom of summer that will never die.
My mum is the depths of the beautiful blue sea.
My mum is the ripest fruit upon every tree.
And that is why she is so special to me.

Kara Wright (11)

My Favourite Person Is My Grandma

My favourite person is my grandma
We love each other lots
Always having a good laugh
Painting lots of dots.

We're always having fun together
Being in the sunshine
We're always playing tennis
Having a good time.

We're always spending time together
Down at Great Grandma's grave
We always help each other
And are very brave.

We like to be near calm, still water
Listening to it trickle
Down the hills and mountainside
Look at it twinkle.

We really love it at Christmas time
Watching the robin's nest
Looking at the snow falling
Watching beyond the crest.

We stay up and watch the new year
Watching the dazzling lights
Listening to Big Ben ringing
Lighting up the night.

Kayleigh Hopcroft (11)

Uncle Brian

My uncle, Brian, is a really fun guy
He always makes me laugh and sometimes makes me cry.
He's always in the mood for some yummy, yummy food,
Like rabbit, pheasant and kangaroo.
But best of all he loves me and I love him too.

Saoirse Yardley (11)

My Favourite Person

My favourite person is as luminous as the sun
My favourlte person is as humorous as a clown
My favourite person is as amiable as a rabbit in a farm
My favourite person is as rapid as a motorbike

My favourite person is as lanky as a mountain
My favourite person is as phenomenal as a pop star
My favourite person is as sweet as candy can be
My favourite person is as lustrous as a star

My favourite person is inconspicuous like a baby asleep
My favourite person is as loquacious as a teacher
My favourite person is as luscious as a strawberry
My favourite person is as alluring as a bride

My favourite person is as astute as a mathematician
My favourite person is as grown up as an adult
My favourite person is like the beautiful smell of roses
My favourite person is like the mouth watering taste of the juicy, colourful fruits I pick off the trees

My favourite person is as kind and sweet as an innocent puppy
My favourite person is as gentle as a flower
My favourite person is as happy as a frog
My favourite person is the colour yellow

My favourite person is filled with pleasure
My favourite person is my friend
My favourite person is a super, shining star!

Kalsey Herian (10)

My Best Friend

My best friend will be there for you
When you fall down and lose your shoe.
Some people will laugh at you,
But my best friend will be there for you.

April John (10)

Lily

I have this little puppy named Lily
She's cute, cuddly and quite silly
Even though she may bite
And gives visitors a fright
Deep inside she's really quite frilly.

Her big brown eyes
Will soften the hardest of guys
And she's so cute she is on a Christmas card
Her big, floppy ears will surely bring tears
To even the rulers of Baghdad.

One day a little boy named John
Came to play with my younger brother Tom
Lily ran up to greet him
All she wanted to do was play
But John wouldn't have it . . .
He screamed and ran away.

Now I love Lily
She's gentle and she's kind
But be very, very wary
When she's got a wild look in her eye
All the kindness goes away
All gentleness forgotten
She'll jump at you from behind
And bite you on the bottom.

Matthew Wilson (11)

My Friend

I have a friend, her name is Zoe
But instead I call her Z O E
I have a friend creative and fun
Who likes to dance all day long
I have a friend who is sweet and kind
She's the best friend for mankind.

Elleanor Rearie (9)

My Favourite Person

I'm going to write about my brother Moses
We always go on adventures.
We even go to funfairs, parks and dungeons.
Of course the best one was bungee jumping,
And he always makes my heart go pumping.
When we eat he's like a monster
But to me he's just another person.
When we go to the park he loves playing tennis
But his secret is watching Dennis the Menace.
He always does good crosses in football,
But you know him, big and strong and plays dodgeball.
I'm always going to love my brother,
He's always going to make me hover.
He has an addiction to play on the Xbox
But he always buys his shoes from Reebok.
I'll always love my brother Moses
He will make your eyes open and close
At seven o'clock we always have our dinner,
And after he always calls me the Binner.
At football he always wears a hood,
You'll think he's bad but he's good.
He'll always be my best brother,
But I do love my mother.
I love my brother Moses,
And that's the end of that.

Sabir Assad Amin (10)

Mam And Dad

My mam makes me happy
And makes me laugh
Mam makes me smile every single day.

Dad is good at tickling though
And gives the best cuddles
Dad is the best, so is my mam.

Natasha Medcalf (6)

Forever

You're such a thoughtful person,
So lovely and so kind,
And friends as special as you
Are very hard to find.

When I look in your eyes
You know what is wrong,
You are always there for me
When I need you to be.

This is why I wrote this poem,
Because I love you very much,
And when I read this poem
It reminds me that . . .

I will stay with you forever,
Even when we die,
Because friends as special as you
Are very hard to find.

I am glad I found a friend as special as you
Because if I didn't, I would be stuck
And wouldn't know what to do.
So I'm very glad I found you,
And glad you found me too.
Best friends forever,
Such as me and *you!*

Abigail Harris (11)

My Favourite Person

M y mum is my favourite person because she plays with me a lot.
Y ou don't know what's she's like with photos, Mum takes them everywhere.

M um makes me confident in everything I do.
U sually Mum takes me swimming, it's great.
M um is caring and fun!

Serena Piacentini (9)

Because She Makes Me Tea

I have lots of games
I have a cat
I have lots of clothes
I even have a hat

My games are fun
But I finish them quickly
My cat purrs at me
But she can't make tea

My clothes are cool
They make me look good
And my hat is cool
And it saves me from wearing a hood

I love my things
That were bought for me
By my favourite person in the world
My mummy

I love my mum
And appreciate her
She spends all her time
With my sisters and me

I love her so much
Because she makes me tea.

Jessica Foskett (15)

Parents

P arents are my favourite people
A lways know what to do when I'm having problems
R espect is what they give to me and I give it back to them
E verything I do, they make sure I'm safe
N ever let me do things that are dangerous
T ell me how to do the things I don't know how to do
S o supportive of the things I do.

Kelvin Ihama (9)

The Funny Friend Of Mine

She always laughs,
I always laugh,
We always laugh together,
Ha, ha, ha, ha!

We always play tag,
We never drop our bag,
We love to play together!
We always laugh together!

She's brown and I'm white,
My hair is dark and hers is light.
My eyes are black and hers are brown,
She likes rum and I like gum!

We are different but she's my friend,
We feel the same,
Though I'm white and she's brown.
We could be sisters,
She and me!

She tells me secrets and I tell her mine.
She plays with me and I play with her.
She reads my eyes and I read hers!

We always laugh together,
Ha, ha, ha, ha, ha, ha!

Ee Von Foo (9)

My Mum

My mum is my hero.
She's a hero because
She's been there for me
And looked after me
When I was young,
And still looks after me now,
And she loves me forever.

Zenani Johnson (12)

The Mission

When the house is still and silent
And everyone's asleep
There's one little creature that's not
Nibbles takes a leap
She's a very unusual hamster
That works on missions through nights
She can do the monkey bars
And turn off bedroom lights
One night she had a big mission
The greatest of them all
She parachuted down the stairs
And didn't even fall
It was then she came to realise
That there was sadness in the air
She used up all her strength
And got back up the stairs
She saw my crying
Only half-asleep
She used her last bit of energy
And gave a final leap
She nuzzled into me
And I gave her a watery smile
Nibbles is my favourite person
She'd be in my favourite things pile.

Sally Lancaster (10)

Friends Are There

F riends are to share
R emembering each day
I n a special way
E ven though they are far away
N ever look down
D on't have a frown . . .
'Cause friends are always there.

Verity Fretwell (11)

Who Is My Favourite Person?

Who is my
favourite person I
really can't decide is
it my fish or family
members or anyone
I find? I haven't
got the
slightest
clue, maybe
it's even you.
This is such a
hard decision
to find the
right person
as they all
have different
reasons to be
my favourite one
but I have come
to a conclusion

that it's
definitely
everyone!

Emma Reeves (11)

My Sister

My sister is friendly, but not to me,
She loves me a lot, as much as I love sweet tea.
But she can get fierce and furious,
Not as much as I get curious.
She yells a lot,
But I tell her to stop.
I don't think you want to know,
Sorry, it's the end of the show.

Lathan Mahalingam (11)

My Favourite Person Is Michael Jackson

Michael Jackson, the king of pop
Whose feet would never stop
Who loved to sing
'Billy Jean' and glitter sparkling
In his team.
Michael Jackson who cared about nations
That we are all equal despite our colours.
The king of pop, the creator of 'Thriller'
Who is known by millions of fans
But his only love was for us to unite
And to be a better world.
Man in the mirror
Man in the mirror
Who really cares about beings?
Man in the mirror
Man in the mirror
That can change our ways
Man in the mirror
Man in the mirror
Let's watch our ways around things
We are not the same but we can
Live this way if we put more effort into it
RIP.

Phoebean Olanrewaju (10)

My Favourite Person Is My Mother

M is for the million things she gave me
O means only that she's growing old
T is for the tears shed to save me
H is for her loving heart
E is for her eyes that watch over me
R is for she always tells me the right thing.

Put that all together and that spells 'Mother',
That word means the world to me.

Fola Taiwo (10)

Someone Special

I love this person, yes it's true,
When I'm with her I smile all day through.
She'll make me laugh, but won't make me cry,
She's the best, here are eight reasons why:
She's funny,
She's caring,
She's ever so kind,
When I need someone there for me
She's right by my side,
She's pretty,
She's thoughtful,
She's lovely as well,
She makes me feel better
When I'm feeling unwell.

Can you guess who it is yet?
I'll give you some clues.
She's older than me
And probably older than you too,
She pays all the bills only just in time,
And if something goes wrong, she makes it fine.

There are no more clues as I've given you some,
It's ever so easy, this person is . . . *my mum.*

Chloe Nicklin (11)

My Favourite Person 2009

My teacher is called Miss Jones
She always laughs and never moans
If my class is good all day
She will often give us extra play

She gives us lots of good books to read
And teaches us all the Welsh words we need
That's why she's great; she is the best
Miss Jones stands out from all the rest!

Lois Type (10)

My Big Sis

My favourite person is my big sis,
There's never a concert that she'll miss.

My sister's the best,
She's better than the rest.

Sometimes when I'm cut and bruised
She'll give me a hot chocolate and a long cruise.

My sister's the best,
She's better than the rest.

When it's rainy outside and there's nothing to do,
We'll all gather round for a game of Doctor Who.

My sister's the best,
She's better than the rest.

She's always thinking of fun things to do,
Like having a picnic or going to the zoo.

My sister's the best,
She's better than the rest.

And best of all, when sports day's here,
She always gives me a big fat cheer.

My sister's the very best!

Sumayyah Iqbal (10)

My Favourite Person

My favourite person isn't a person but I suppose it doesn't matter
She's a dog, her name is Tangle. Tangle by name and nature
Her fur is brown, her eyes are big and her fur is very tangled
My favourite person is a dog. The best dog in the world.

My favourite person has four legs and is very small
She barks at cats, barks at dogs and barks at horses too
She has big ears, a black nose and patronises the rabbit
My favourite person is a dog. The best dog in the world.

Toby Maitland (11)

You

(A poem dedicated to Mum)

There is no one like you,
You're there for me,
And without you,
Where would I be?

There is no one like you,
You love and care for me,
And without you,
Where would I be?

There is no one like you,
You're warm and kind to me,
And without you,
Where would I be?

There is no one like you,
You inspire and encourage me,
And without you,
Where would I be?

So listen to my message,
Because where would I be,
Without you being there,
And you loving me?

Emily Baldwin (11)

My Funny Brother

I have a funny brother
He's only three years old
When he was a baby
He looked as if he was bald

Now he's tall and slender
And fair upon his head
He's turned into a monkey
And drives me round the bend.

Lucy MacKenzie (8)

Larry

My favourite person is Cousin Larissa,
But just for short I call her Larry.
When I'm not with her,
I really do miss her.

I see her has a good role model
As she works hard and doesn't mind a bit of graft.
She's not afraid to get her hands dirty,
Because she wants a million before she's thirty.
She worked hard at school,
She's sensible, mature and nobody's fool.

She lives an active and full social life,
She has lots of hobbies like football,
Running and motorbike riding.

She really loves animals, as I do too,
She has a loopy dog called Ted
And a hamster with no name,
Who's not right in the head.

I would like to tell you more
But the space is limited, as you are aware,
But if I have any problems, I know she'll be there.
Love you, Larry.

Lillie-Mai Reilly (11)

My Dog Really Is The Best

My dog, Bobby, is my number one
A truly top dog
My dog, Bobby, is a hairy lump of fun
Who jumps up at me like a frog.

Bobby walks with me through the park
Lays beside me when I sleep
He talks to me with his bark
And loves to chew his feet.

Jodie Smith (10)

My Little Sister

My little sister is the best person in the world
She works very hard to keep everyone happy

My sister may be diabetic
There's one thing for sure she's as strong as brick

She's always got a smile on her face
And never ever loses her place

We are nothing like each other
And don't look like our mother

She is five-years-old
And is very, very bold

She loves our rabbits in the back garden
Even when she drops their food
She never goes in a mood

Her favourite colour's pink
And she can only just reach the sink

She maybe a pain in the butt
But she never cries a lot when she gets a cut

My little sister is the best person in the world
And she always will be.

Martha Okon (12)

Mia

My dog, Mia, is so great,
She loves to lay in the sun and bake.
She barks as soon as she hears a sound,
The postman, the binmen, on their round.
When it's windy her big ears flap,
When it rains she looks like a rat.
My dog, Mia, is so great,
I wouldn't be without her,
She's my mate.

Matteo Sarro (11)

Magical Sister

My favourite person is a family member,
Which is Amna, my super sister.
She's also my best friend,
Our friendship will never end.
Sometimes we argue and fight,
But she's my sister so it's alright.

She's my favourite person because she's so fun,
Sometimes we have picnics under the sun.
Sometimes she even bakes
Delicious biscuits and belly-rumbling cakes.

Now she lives in Cardiff, 200 miles from me,
She lives quite close to the sea.
She sends me things with her magical powers (or the post)
And she's the one who I love most.
Her powers are being a brilliant sister
And she's mine, so don't steal her.

No matter how far apart we are
She will always be my favourite by far (aww).
Most children think sisters are a pest,
But I think that mine's totally the best,
Better than all the rest!

Aasia Majid (10)

My Mum

My mum is really great
We act as if we're best mates
My mum cares for me
We are as happy as could be
My mum loves me
She's the whole world to me
As you can see we're really close
I could go on forever
But I've got to go!

Rebecca Whiting (12)

My Sister, Georgina

My sister laughs with me,
She has sensitive ears and
High noises freak her out.

She is not just any sister, she is my sister.
When we go on rides,
We always go on the Twister.

Georgina loves stories of horror,
But when it comes to money,
She always wants to borrow.

My sister is wildlife-friendly
And loves wildlife.
She has a wonderful life.

Me and her love to make cakes together,
Especially licking out the bowl after.
We go on the computer together
And the room fills with laughter.

Georgina is autistic
And sometimes finds life hard,
But I will always love her
And be her bodyguard.

Dominic Starkey (11)

My Cat

My cat has immense paws
The size of boxing gloves in fat
With prickly claws sprouting out each side.

My cat has hair as soft as velvet
And endless whiskers that tickle you.

My cat has bulky eyes which are useful for hunting
As well as its occupational muzzle!

My cat is purrrrfect!

Bobbie Smith (11)

My Best Friend

I look at her and she grins
From our friends, we are hiding
Behind the bins.

We have played a joke
Which they don't get
But we are in hysterics
Cos it was funny, you bet.

She has an angel face
But there's a devil inside
For she is very cheeky -
Every trick she has tried.

We always stick together, never seen apart
She is naughty, but caring
And has a very big heart.

Her face is always glowing with happiness and fun
And we have the best time of all
When the school day is done.

She is also sensible, all problems she mends
Always knows what to do
Which is why she is my very best friend.

Rosie Margolis (12)

Who Is He?

Who is he, who could this be?
It's someone who is special to me.

Who is he, who could this be?
This is someone rather important to me.

Who is he, who could this be?
He's someone I am proud of actually.

Who is he, who could this be?
He is my favourite cousin, Sam, as you can see!

Angie Choudhury (9)

Alasdair

My favourite person ought to be
My little brother, who is three,
While his name is Alasdair,
So is his soft toy cuddly bear.
We play outside when it is sunny,
He's very cute and very funny.
We play with toys and make them talk,
He makes them play and makes them walk.
We build snowmen in the snow,
Make biscuits out of cookie dough.
We watch TV and play at the park,
We ride our bikes and camp out in the dark.
We play pretend and both dress up,
Have a teddy bear picnic with toy tea cups,
And when I'm feeling lonely and sad,
He makes me feel not so bad.
He'll cheer me up with a made-up dance,
He'll jump about and laugh and prance.
My little brother will never bore,
But soon he's going to be four.
Although he is growing up fast,
I hope our fun will always last.

Heather Jeffrey (11)

My Beloved Dog

He was cute in a way,
He was well-trained
And did what you say.
He was a good little dog
All the way.

So hip hip hooray!
Hip hip hooray!
Hip hip hooray
For Jake!

Lucy Card (9)

My Favourite Person - A Shining Star

Genevieve

Genevieve is special,
Genevieve is kind
And with her stunning red hair,
She is not hard to find.

Genevieve is caring,
Genevieve is great,
She is also the kind
Of person you could never hate.

Genevieve is clever,
Genevieve doesn't rhyme,
She always has good ideas,
Well, most of the time.

I'm glad Genevieve is my cousin,
But she is very far away,
Which means I can't visit her,
Every single day.

Genevieve is my favourite person
Because of all these reasons,
She will always be my favourite,
No matter what the seasons.

Anna Nelson (10)

My Mother

M y mother is wonderful in so many ways,
Y oung and graceful.

M ind-reading skills (scary).
O nly the greatest in the world.
T here is only one person like my mum,
H eavenly and beautiful.
E arly bird (waking up at 5.50).
R eally my mum is number one,
    or as I like to call her, Supermum.

Hope Newman (11)

My Best Friend

My best friend is called Sarah
She's laughable, funny and kind
So she's my favourite person -
And she doesn't mind.

We have similar things in common
And play with each other every day
Plus, if we're sad and lonely
'Come and play with me,' we'd say.

We're always partners in class
And lways do work together
We have got other friends to play with
But me and Sarah we'll be friends forever.

I've been round her house
And she's been round mine
We know each other off by heart
Ever since we were nine!

So she's my favourite person
And my best friend
We'll keep on going
But this poem will end!

Beth Robinson (10)

Aaron Lennon

My favourite player running down the wing,
He's the super fast skilful king.
One day I hope to be like him,
Walking down the tunnel, greeting all my fans.
Even having time to give a wave to my nans.
Shirt, shorts and football boots on.
Wembley and White Hart Lane are where I belong.
So thank you Aaron for showing me the way
And hopefully soon I will make it one day.

Callum O'Reilly (10)

My Favourite Person - A Shining Star

I Love My Mum

My favourite person
Is my mum
School plays and things
She is sure to come

She buys me presents
When I am good
If I could change her
I never would

My bedroom is full
It is crammed with stuff
My mums says I have too much
I don't think I have enough

When I do well at school
We all go out for dinner
When we play games
I'm always a winner

When I get homework
It's always done
Thanks to the help of
My wonderful mum.

Alex Wood (9)

My Favourite Person - Anthony

My brother Anthony is only two
And he copies everything that I do,
When I wake up he is in my room
So we go downstairs to watch cartoons.
When that's over we go outside,
I play football and he is by my side.
I sometimes think that he's a pest,
But really I know that Anthony is the best,
That's my favourite person and brother, Anthony.

Ben Finn (11)

My Crazy Mum

I will tell you a story about my mum,
She is so embarrassing, but so much fun.
She loves to sing, she sings so loud,
But that's my mum and I'm still proud.

In the summer holidays it was really hot
So we filled up the paddling pool right to the top.
My mum came running, we shouted, 'Don't crash!'
But it was too late, she made a big splash!

When my friends come round after school
She tries to act really cool.
I say to her, 'Mum, give it a rest,'
But I soon realise that she is the best.

We were at the school disco one Friday night,
She wore her trousers a bit too tight.
She got up to dance and wiggle her hips
But, 'Oh no!' I cried when her trousers split!

But even though she makes me cringe,
I know I shouldn't moan and whinge.
I tell her loads so she won't forget,
That she's the best mummy I could ever get.

Sophie Glandfield (10)

My Favourite Person

My favourite person is Zach,
He is my little brother.
He is very playful and
Loves to do lots of art.
Zach likes the colour gold
And loves to eat chicken.
The thing I like about Zach
Is that he always keeps me happy.
That is why my favourite person is Zach.

Ben Pearce (10)

My Great Grandmother

My favourite person in the world
Is my great grandmother
And I know if you'd meet her
You'd also love her

She's not old and bent and wrinkly
As you might think
She's young and jolly and lively
Always with a smile and wink

Her birthdays are magic - for she becomes younger
In spirit and in mind
But her body is not keeping up with her
To her it's not too kind

I love her hair-raising stories
Of when she was young
She was really naughty
But pretends to be a hero unsung

She's loving and kind and generous
And joins us in our tricks
We all fight to go to her
Cos she gives us the kicks.

Pessi Frankel (11)

Grandad!

I love going on walks
And having fun talks with my grandad
I love doing sports
And getting taught Spanish by my grandad
I love going sailing
And never failing with my grandad
I love Twin Lakes
And eating lots of cakes with my grandad
My favourite person is my grandad!

Lauren Grace Gallacher (9)

My Cat!

My favourite person isn't really a person,
He is, in fact, a cat.
A very fluffy, furry friend,
Not a bat, or a rat!

My cat is very tabby,
No, he isn't plain,
He is very brown,
The pattern is insane!

In the morning he jumps through the window,
No cat flap on the door,
He just scratches on the side and in he comes,
Then he lands on the bathroom floor!

His name is Oscar,
But he's no award,
No, definitely not,
But he's like a cat lord!

He loves his food, my cat,
Fed every morning and night.
He munches it up like a vulture.
Oh, when he feeds it's a sight!

Amber Madden (10)

My Great Mate Bro

We've known each other since we were three
When we started nursery
Shared laughs and tears, books and toys
Now we're older it's boys, boys, boys!
Sleepovers, makeovers, yours or mine
No matter what we will always make time
Sometimes we argue, but always let it go
Long live the fun,
My great mate Bro!

Ruby Haggie

My Little Brother

As funny as a joke
All fizzy like Coke

Daring and naughty
Competitive, sporty

Cheeky little monkey
Thinks R&B's funky

Kind and caring
Sensitive, sharing

A bright bouncy ball
So compact and small

As smart as a fox
As smelly as socks

As quick as a flea
To the top of a tree

Shines like the stars
Mad about cars

Excellent giggle and fabulous grin
He's my little brother and I love him.

Megan Phoenix (12)

My Baby Sister

My baby sister is very, very cute
She smiles all day and she makes me too
She makes me laugh and she makes me wiggle
But best of all she makes me giggle
She's my favourite person, oh yes it's true
My little baby sister, my beautiful Boo Boo
She is my sister, I love her so
I am so glad she is there to make me glow
You all are wondering just who she is
She's my sister, Katie, oh yes she is.

Kerri-Ann Middleton (11)

My Favourite Person

Lurking behind the dark veil
Of every human is a person
A person of great creativity and insight
Of great beauty, strength and reliability
My imagination!

My imagination
Is like a slave just waiting to be freed
An innocent prisoner awaiting justice
It is like a father waiting for the news of a child
Like a miner that just struck gold.

My imagination
Is much more than just imagining
It is like you are in a whole new world
Where you can decide
And create everyone and everything.

Without my imagination
And that sense of creativity in me
I wouldn't be me
And that is why I will always be proud
To call it *my favourite person!*

Somto Egboga (11)

Untitled

I love my mammy, she is the best,
Mammy calls me her little princess.
My mammy makes me laugh and smile,
And she always cuddles me when I cry.
I love my mammy's sausages and chips,
When I finish, I lick my lips.
When it's night-time I go to bed,
My mammy and me say our prayers.
Before I close my eyes at night,
One thing is said, and that's goodnight.

Katelyn John (6)

The Quest To Find The Best

With you . . .
Not a depressing moment flows by,
Not a flower stops growing,
Not a millimetre of confidence going.
Just a smile coming from miles,
Down, down, safely landing on the ground.

A pretty person,
Fair, smooth skin,
Soft, long hair,
Being kept with care.
Natural beauty
Is the key to success.

Who is this person,
Have you guessed?
I'll give you a clue,
She is the *best!*

It's the end of the quest,
So who do you think is my best?
My mum!
She is simply the chosen number one!

Anisah Bulsari (11)

My Cousin Danielle

Danielle died on the first of July
And I never got to say goodbye.
My eyes, they fill up with tears,
My heart will always be broken,
I think of her each day and night.
Her pearly-white smile was a beautiful slight.
I know she's watching over me!
Through the stars to her I see.
One day I'm sure we'll meet again,
My cousin, friend, we'll feel no pain.

Sasha Moore (10)

My Favourite Person, My Grandad

When I think of my grandad, I feel a warm glow,
He will always be there, that I know.

Always people ask me,
What my grandad does,
That has such an effect on me,
I simply reply;

'My grandad, he's so witty and wise,
He tells me never to give up
Because he always tries.

My grandad, he's so honest, sincere and true,
He always makes me chuckle,
Whenever I'm feeling blue.

My grandad, forever hard-working and loving,
Devoted to my granny, who is very brave,
It lightens his heart, to brighten up her day.

Although he works his socks off
Grandad knows how to play
I'll never forget that fairground ride,
Us laughing all the way.'

Rosie Scott (10)

My Best Friend

My best friend is as thin as a stick
He has loads of money and his name is Nick.
Nick's blaring roar is against the law
He has a colossal paw which is as big as a spiky saw!
Nick is as tall as a gigantic tower
Nick also has lots of tremendous power!
His hiccups make everyone trip up
He smells of rotten eggs
Which gives everyone tired legs.
Nick has many good qualities
He is kind and full of generosity.
Nick is also funny and makes everyone
Hold their sides with laughter
And he loves chasing bunnies.
That's Nick, my mischievous cat,
Who tries to sneak fish from the pond,
He likes watching James Bond.
Nick also stops thieves from robbing banks,
He steals from the rich and gives to the poor.
That's Nick, my best tabby cat,
And he always will be!

Philip Vergis Mathew (10)

My Favourite Person

My favourite person is not family, but friend
And I hope that our friendship
Will never, ever end.

We could talk all day
Until the blinds go down
And when she's being funny
She acts like a clown.

Although she's far away
In a completely different school
I know even when we're parted
That our friendship will stay cool.

So however big the gap is
Before I see her again
I know Hope won't forget me
And I will not refrain.

From asking her to meet me
In the park or at the shops
The best thing I could say to her is,
'Hopey, you're the tops!'

Megan Jones (11)

Daddy And Mummy

Daddy
My dad is special
And whenever I'm feeling down
His smile always cheers me up
And he is always there to help me
He supports me and cares about me.

Mummy
My mum is very kind and caring
She helps round the house
And tries to make everything fun.

Jonathan Baker (10)

A Girl's Best Friend!

My dog's name is Tess,
She is a very good friend,
Me and her have a relationship that
Will never ever end.

She likes to run and chase a ball,
She likes to chew on wood,
Sometimes she is a naughty girl
But most of the time she's good.

She plays with me in the morning,
Until I got to bed,
I'm supposed to dream of chocolate,
But I dream of her instead.

When I am sad she comes and sits by me,
She also gives me a kiss
Which is very slobbery.

We got her from a rescue centre,
To give her a new home,
She likes to eat, she likes to play
She'll never be alone.

Maddy Baker (10)

My Favourite Person - My Mummy

My favourite person is my mummy
Because I came out of her tummy.
She held me tight when I got kicked by my brother
And that is why I love to call her Mother.
She tucks me into bed at night,
And sorts me out when I look a fright.

My mummy hasn't got a man to love,
But to me she's an angel sent from the heavens above.
She took me on a trip to Florida and Turkey too
But there's nothing more special than for me to hear her say, 'I love you.'

Amber Throop (10)

My Dog

My favourite person?
Well to be honest
I don't know.

Sometimes I think it's my mum
Sometimes my dad
Sometimes my best friend.

But parents don't always understand you
And friends aren't friends forever
But they're something that will
Love, care and understand you.

You love them but sometimes you think they don't notice
But they do
His nickname is 'man's best friend'
And it's true.

He's your dog
No matter how angry you get
No matter how hard the times
He loves you forever
That's why he's my best friend.

Rebecca Turnbull (12)

My Mum

S ometimes she makes me annoyed
U nderstands me all the time
S he's a super cook
A wonderful mum to have
N ice and kind all the time

L ovely looking
A lso a super mum
R emembers the things I like
B uys me lots of goodies
Y ou may not like her, but I love her to bits!

Scarlet Larby (9)

My Friend Hazel

I have a friend called Hazel
She is really sweet
We play with each other so much
We even forget to eat.

I have a friend called Hazel
She is really kind
We go on the computer so much
It nearly makes us blind.

I have a friend called Hazel
She is really cool
We like each other so much
We even see each other in school.

I have a friend called Hazel
We have lots of fun
Her brother always wants to join us
But we get up and run.

Hazel is a friend; good, sweet and kind,
If you knew her
You wouldn't take her out of your mind.

Maqdus Iqbal (9)

My Favourite Person

My favourite person, that's got to be my dad
Although at times he can be quite mad

He takes us on long bike rides
Usually to bird hides
And always keeps us on the go

But when he is full of stress
You *do not* want to mess
With the man on a Friday night

Oh and did I mention that my favourite person is my dad!

Christy Duvenhage (11)

Yaya

(Yaya: Greek for Grandmother)

Yaya was her name . . .
She's not here,
I can't call her name.

Her hair was red,
Her eyes were blue,
She made me smile, it was so true.

We had lots of fun,
Doing different things in the sun,
She liked her holidays, clothes and shoes,
She also liked a glass of wine, too.

She made me cakes
And taught me how to rhyme.
She made me laugh,
All of the time.

Yaya died in Jan '09,
She was so special it made me cry.
I close my eyes, I see her there,
And now we are all in despair.

Ben Gregoriou (11)

Joey

Joey is my little brother
But he's not like any other
Joey may only be three
But he's special to me
He likes to laugh and play
All through the day
Joey loves me a lot
And I love him just the same
That's why he's my favourite little brother
And I'll never forget his name.

Yolanda Quartey (9)

A Poem About Michael Jackson, The King Of Pop

I'm so sad you have reached your death.
All the fame that will be left.

You will always win,
You are especially known to sing.

Those memories that will be found
Although you make no sound

We are all so sad,
Some people are even mad.

Oh please come back,
Though that may be impossible to reach that.

I'm really sad you're not there
I always know that you will always still care.

Oh, what else can I say?
I'm so sad every day.
You are my favourite person, you see,
And your music will always be special to me.

Alexandria Allan-Sutcliffe (8)

My Favourite Person

G randmother is beautiful and kind
R aven Avenue is where she lives with her very big mind
A n angel from Heave is what she is, no sins
N ever call her bad because she clears out her bins
D iligent at writing and as happy as can be
M onday express is her time to be seen
O h she is wonderful and proud
T here is the countryside with not one cloud
H er fine voice and her little house
E lephants are on all the streets
'R est,' she says to me, 'and you will get some treats.'

Sebastian Zahn (10)

My Mum

My mum is sweet
My mum is special
In every single way.

I know with her
I'll be safe from harm
Every single day.

My mum is smart
And fun, but still
Listens to every word I say.

I make a mess
As I play but I know
Mum will pack away.

My mum is really cool
But she still knows
How to act the fool.

My mum is really, really great
She let's me stay up
Gone past eight!

Georgia Franks (10)

Mother, Mother

Mother, mother
You are like no other
When I am down
You turn that frown upside down
You provide me with food
You provide me with shelter
You provide me with what I need to live forever
Without you my life is incomplete
If you aren't here I feel defeat
When you are here I feel fine
You make me feel like a ray of sunshine.

Dayo Nylander (11)

A Cat Called Giorgio

It takes five strokes to make my cat purr,
Then he's all over me,
But not like Armani who belongs to Fleur,
Because Armani is always asleep.
No cat is like Giorgio as his actions flow in a gentle manner
And fur, so soft and healthy.
I remember on his fifth birthday,
Lots of balloons and a big banner.
As we celebrated, Giorgio wore a plastic crown
And looked so wealthy.
He'll graciously catwalk along to the cat bed,
But because he's so precise, Giorgio
Likes to sniff around for a comfortable position.
His nose twitches, then he'll rest his head.
Going to sleep is his final daily decision,
Time to go to bed . . .
The reason he is my best pal
Is because of his personality.
Lively like a parrot, he is.
I love him and Giorgio loves me.

Chloe Verebelyi (10)

My Mum Is The Best

My mum is the best
She does the cooking and the cleaning
And she plays with me
She is the best.

She helps me with my homework
She puts on cool movies
She makes me laugh
And she makes me smile
We have lots of fun
I love my mum
She is the best.

Kiara Knight (9)

My Dog, Jasper

My dog, Jasper,
Is a disaster.
He is a bundle of fun
And he can run.
He likes to make a din,
He also likes to win.

My dog, Jasper,
Is a disaster.
He runs up and down
All over the town.
He is black and white
But he is not a fright.

My dog, Jasper,
Is a disaster,
He rolls around
On the ground.
He is very jolly
Because he is a collie
And I love him!

Charlotte Selby (11)

My Brother Jay

M ost of the time he's a pain
Y oung, smart and funny

B rothers, many people have them
R ubbish at singing but he's my hero
O nly annoying all the time
T ough, I don't think so but he does
H eart like a soldier, brave
E very now and then we have a fight
R ocking and rolling all the time, he's my rock star
    Still I love him so much
    Jay, I love you.

Sadie Colley (11)

My Aunty Gillina

I love my aunty, she's the best one I've got.
She loves me too, she loves me a lot.
She cooks stew in a big, big pot
And she's hoping soon to be getting a baby cot.

My aunty, Gillina, is funny and nice,
To me she's better than Ginger Spice.
She taught me to cook a risotto with white rice.
She will never, ever dislike going skating on ice.

Some people call her 'G' for short.
She has never been bad to have had to go to court.
She's been so many times to the airport.
When she counts backwards she ends with nought.

My aunty, Gillina, is someone who speaks her mind,
Although she is never, ever unkind.
She helps me with my homework when I'm behind,
She's still at her job and hasn't yet resigned.

I dedicate this to her because
She's my favourite person and I love her to bits.

Dayna Cook (11)

My Favourite Person

I have this friend, a magnificent friend,
Who keeps on driving me round the bend!

She sings too much, that's her problem,
And she keeps on hanging out with *them.*

But she's a good soul, she's hard to forget,
In a matter of fact she's better than that!

I'll always remember the times we spent together,
In rain or shine no matter the weather.

So no matter what she does and no matter what she says,
We will always, always be best friends.

Kristina Werner (10)

My Favourite Person

My favourite person is my mum
Even though she's very dull,
She cheers me up when I feel bum,
My favourite person is my mum.

She's very caring and kind
And is always on my mind,
I never want to see her hurt
Because she puts her hands in the dirt.
My favourite person is my mum.

She's very busy doing things
But she still has time for me,
She'll talk me through my problems
If I'm feeling hurt.
My favourite person is my mum.

She buys me clothes and gives me food,
She gave me my life.
My favourite person is my mum.

No one's as good as my mum.

Evie Bull (8)

JD My Best Friend

My favourite person is my dog,
JD is her name,
Loyalty is her aim
She will never give you any shame,
Only friendship you shall gain.

JD is very strong,
She will lick you with her tongue,
Her bark is like a song,
You shall enjoy her forever long,
She will never be in the wrong,
That is why I love her.

Kyle Wilkinson (12)

Beyoncé

I like her style,
I love her clothes,
She's my favourite person, I suppose.
She can dance and she can sing,
I just love it in 'Single Ladies'
When she struts and does her thing.
When she gets on that stage,
Boy she can dance.
If I was at her concert
I would jump at her
As soon as I got the chance.
Her heels are high,
As well as her career.
If I ever met her,
Oh, how speechless I would be.
Anyone who gets in her way,
How much I feel sorry for them
To me Beyoncé is a star
And the crème de la crème!

Jaydene Reece-Gardner (11)

Joe

Joe is my brother, to him I am like another mother.
I don't like going to school and leaving him,
But I know it's worthwhile
Because when I next see him he makes me smile!

I have chosen Joe to be my favourite person of 2009
Because no matter what, he will always be a friend of mine.

Although he is cute and harmless now,
In three years time when he is five
He'll then start to ruin my life!

It doesn't matter how much he gets in my way,
I will love him tomorrow like I did today!

Georgia O'Keeffe (11)

Allah Is My Favourite!

When I am tired and discouraged from fruitless efforts,
Allah knows how hard I have tried.
When I've cried so long and my heart is in anguish,
Allah has counted my tears.
When I'm lonely and my friends are too busy even for a phone call,
Allah is by my side.
When I think I have tried everything and am not sure when to turn,
Allah has a solution.
When nothing makes sense and I am confused or frustrated,
Allah has the answer.
If my outlook is suddenly brighter and I find traces of hope,
Allah has whispered to me.
When things are going well and I have much to be thankful for
Allah has blessed me.
When something joyful has happened and I am filled with life,
Allah has smiled upon me.
When I have a purpose to fulfil and a dream to follow,
Allah has opened my eyes and called me by name.
Whatever I'm facing . . . Allah knows.

Muhhammed Fahed (10)

My Friend!

My friend is really great,
I love her as a mate,
She's really lairy
But sometimes scary.
We go on bikes
And sometimes hikes.

I love my mate
Because she bakes me cakes.
We both like dancing
And prancing all day long.
My friend is really great,
I love her as a mate.

Kelsey Burdell (12)

Gypsy And George

Gypsy, Gypsy what shall I say?
She's as cheeky as an MP's pay!
She makes me smile,
She makes you laugh,
But sometimes she can be pretty daft.
She loves to play hide-and-seek,
And swim in rivers deep.
The only thing I do not like is when she does a stinker on a massive long hike,
But luckily I can get a quick get away on my speedy mountain bike.
There's another dog Henry who's always very friendly,
We take him out in our 4x4 jeep
And when we get back he likes to have a nice long sleep.
He makes you excited,
He makes you happy.
Oh and not forgetting, Henry is a King Charles Spaniel
And his most favourite cuddly toy is named Daniel.
Gypsy and Henry are the best ever dogs,
They like everyone and everyone likes them
(Well nearly!)

India Howard (11)

My Baby Niece

My baby niece is called Summer,
She likes to see her mother.
She plays with her red ball,
Which she bounces off a wall.
My niece likes Dairylea on toast,
And likes blue and yellow posts.
She lives in Leeds,
And Summer does not like peas.

Summer I love you,
Summer I do
When we're apart,
My heart beats for you.

Courtney Gaunt (11)

Mrs Zee, My Favourite T!

Mrs Zee's my favourite teacher,
She's got all the good-looking features,

She makes me smile,
But only for a while,

When it comes to sums,
She thinks they're fun!

I always do adding,
Sometimes even subtracting!

When she tries to get me to learn,
I always misunderstand!

But when I'm in detention,
She always gets my attention.

This year's nearly ending,
I wish when I'm saying this I'm only pretending.

She's always there to help me out,
I really can't stop myself from laughing out loud!

Sonia Bhangal (10)

My Favourite Person

She is my favourite person
She is funny and makes me laugh
She makes yummy food
She has dark brown eyes
Black, thick hair
She is my favourite person

She is my favourite person
She likes to read
She is very smart
She is the youngest in the family
She is a very nice person
She is my favourite person.

Nana Nkyidjour (10)

Grandma, I'll Always Remember You

Grandma, you were there for me every single day
I'd really like to thank you so now I have to say

You were the best I could have wished for
To me you were everything and more

I've known you since I was one day old
You've been with us through hot and cold

Grandma, we will all miss you
The cakes you baked, we'll miss them too

I dreaded the day you had to die
But I have to be strong and try not to cry

I really respect all you have done
I can't believe this day has come

I wish I had the choice to say 'no'
When I was told you had to go

Grandma, I've always loved you
And now I'll always remember you.

Ellie Harrison (11)

My Sister Louise

She's beautiful, kind, gentle and funny.
When she kisses and cuddles me she calls me Sweety or Honey.
She has two black cats called Lumpy and Rug Rugs
Who sit in the bath and play mouse with the bath plug.
When she smiles her face lights up like a lovely summer's day
And her eyes are as blue as the sky in May.
Her hair is blonde and fine,
She washes and combs it all the time.
If I'm ill and don't feel too bright
She snuggles me at night and leaves on my light.

I'd do anything for her so that she knows
I love her to bits from her head to her toes.

Charlie Mitchell (10)

My Favourite Person

My favourite person is small and kind
She's funny and friendly and one of a kind
She's pretty and blonde, goddess-like too
Her eyes glisten browny-blue
My favourite person is not just that to me
She's my best friend and she's named Evie.

We laugh and joke and have lots of fun
To me she is my number one
She may be Twilight crazy
And extremely lazy
But that doesn't mean a thing to me
Cos she's the bestest friend anyone could ever have.

She has a secure place in my heart
Which no one could ever tear apart
She fills my days with happiness and laughter
Our adventures we go on are just a disaster
But in the end we always have fun
That's why Evie is my number one.

Hannah Greenstreet (14)

My Favourite Person

She is a beautiful butterfly fluttering through the sky.
As comforting as a water bed,
Cuddling me up close as to not hurt me.
She is a fancy limousine - slow but graceful.
And as useful as a pretty handbag ,
Always open for a quick secret.
She is a chocolate fountain oozing with affectionate love
And is as happy as the colour yellow that never darkens.
She is a love film in action, cameras rolling at all times
And as exotic as a fine mango, always up for something different.
She represents glorious weather.
She is my nan!

Ellie McGann (12)

My Favourite Person

My favourite person
Who could that be?
I have a younger brother
Whom I adore
But messes up my room
And pinches my sweets

I have lots of friends
At dance class and school
Bella, Caitlin, Ellie and Phe
Just to mention a few
They're all pretty cool

My favourite person
Now who could that be?
It's harder than I thought
To choose one in particular
You know what
I've decided,
It's *me!*

Jessica Finley (8)

Me And Dilanne

My favourite person is Dilanne,
An extraordinary girl (with a rather nice tan!)
She talks to me like I'm her fan
'The name's Dilanne - glamorous Dilanne!'
When she was angry I ran . . . and ran!
(Apparently because she was like a madman!)
Veggies and rules she'd love to ban,
Or . . . she'll crumple her face up like my gran!
Me and my sister
Hmm . . .
How about
Me and Dilanne!

Meedia Abid (11)

Who To Choose?

Mum or Dad,
Or someone mad?
My big bro?
Him - no!
Or my cousin,
Or pets by the dozen,
Or my friends from the west?
I must protest!

Only the best is able to work,
Some of my ideas are really berserk!
All of them apart from one,
I'll tell you and then my work is nearly done.

My mum and dad,
They stop me being sad!
They keep me busy and tell me what to do,
And they help me with homework when I've got no clue.
Yes, they are the best,
A ton above all the rest!

Anna Freire Camacho (11)

Two Very Special People!

My very special person's name begins with S,
Can you guess?
Her name's Sara,
She's my loving mum,
She's really, really fun,
And she has a neat bun,
My other very special person's name begins with S,
Can you guess?
His name's Simon,
He's my caring dad,
He's very much like a lad,
And his fashion's very bad.

Elisha Stuckey (9)

King Of Pop

Michael Jackson, the mega superstar
A lot of people worshipped him from afar
Your music was exceptional, so rhythmic and so pure
There will never be another superstar like you for evermore.

You started performing at a very young age
You were only six when you took to the stage
With you at the front and your brothers behind
Nobody knew you were such a unique find.

I have seen and heard all your songs
The tunes are so catchy you have to sing along
My favourite song has to be 'Thriller'
The way the ghosts and ghouls come out is really a chiller.

You lived on Earth for fifty years
When you died we all shed tears
It was the end of an era, the best superstar
We will always remember you wherever you are.

RIP Michael Jackson.

Shams Sair (11)

Zac Effron

His films make me laugh
Some make me cry
To be honest he's a popular guy.

He sings like a star
I adore him from afar.

His basketball skills
Give me the thrills.

His sharp blue eyes really stand out
I love the way his lips really pout.

He's a great celebrity and movie star
But the only thing I can do is adore him from afar.

Leah Georgina Randall (11)

My Mum

She stands in the kitchen
Cooking our roast,
Stirring the pans
And reading the post.

Doing the laundry,
Ironing too,
I do my homework,
Oh what a to-do.

Hovering and dusting
All through the house,
Around me and my sister,
Who's lounging about.

She finishes the cleaning,
Time for a treat,
Spending time together
Is oh so neat,
That's why my mum is so sweet.

Rachel Cunliffe (11)

My Dad's The Coolest

My fantastic dad
Drives me mad.
Me and my dad have lots of fun,
He chases me and I have to run.
When I've got a lollipop, giving it a lick,
If Dad's around, I've got to eat quick.
But he's my dad and I don't care
Because I couldn't find a better one anywhere.
I love him lots, like Jelly Tots.
I'm like his little flower in a plant pot.
He wins me prizes and plans surprises,
Birthdays, Christmas or whenever,
I'll love him forever!

Shannon Richardson (8)

My Grandad

I love my grandad
He's a kinda funny fella,
He thinks he's an amazing storyteller.
He tells me things of years gone by
Like when my dad was a twinkle in his eye.

He does these tricks like taking off his thumb
But at the time when I was young it didn't seem much fun.
He's quite bald now and what's left is all grey
'The wind blew it off one winter's day,' he'd say.

Now in the days of black and white
When my grandad was a lad,
It must have been so boring with no colour,
'Were you sad?'

At first he frowned and then he smiled
And said, 'Sam, you make me laugh
We did have colour in our lives,
Just not on photographs.'

Samantha Griffin (11)

My Mommy

I love the taste of my mommy's cooking
Also she is very good-looking
She is very nice to me
One day she forgot the door key
My mom is fun
And she really loves the sun
We could play all day
And when the day ends
We go to sleep
Wake up and . . .
Play another day
Me and my mom
Together forever.

Deanne Cope (10)

My Mum

My mum means a lot to me
And in this poem you will see,
Why she's my favourite in the family.
Every time I fall down
She's the quickest in the town.

She takes us to really good places
And pulls a lot of funny faces.
She's not that good at running
But she does look quite stunning.

She cooks our tea and cleans after us
But sometimes she makes a fuss.
She buys me clothes, sweets and games,
And is very good at remembering names.

She loves us forever
And will hate us, never.
She's very nice to some,
That's why I love my mum.

Jack Mapstone (10)

My Favourite Person

Miss Lawrence
Is my teacher
She is so kind
And loving
She has fine
Blonde hair
And dances everywhere
Always teaching me
To do my work with glee
She's pretty
And nice
But . . .
She hates mice.

Alicia Price (10)

My Dad

My dad, he's the best
Even in his old string vest
He makes me laugh out loud
I hope I make him proud.

My dad, he's the best
We go on walks and have a rest
We take the dogs to have a run
Me and my dad have lots of fun.

My dad, he's the best
He goes away and I get left
Off he goes on his big boat
I will see him soon when he comes home.

My dad, he's the best
I love him loads
He calls me his toad
He's great, he's my best friend
I love my dad till the end, my dad.

Cameron Barkshire (10)

My Cat Sparky

My cat, Sparky, is as black as midnight
His yellow eyes gleaming like gems
My cat, Sparky, purrs like a tractor
As he settles on my lap to be stroked
My cat, Sparky, loves Felix pouches
And Whiskas, oh so fishy
My cat, Sparky, has a special treat
Licking out the clotted cream tub
My cat, Sparky, is as soft as a pillow
From his velvet paws to the tip of his furry tail
My cat, Sparky, sleeps on my bed
Curling up at my feet
My cat, Sparky, is the best cat in the whole world - usually.

Caitlin Jones (12)

Mummy And Me

Me and my mum
Have lots of fun,
She makes boring exciting,
Even if me and my sister are fighting.

She looks after me,
Makes my tea,
Does my washing,
Takes me shopping
And buys me lots of things!

My mum cooks me food.
When I'm in a mood
She makes me smile
For a while!

She looks pretty
And is really witty.
I listen to her hum.
I love you, Mum.

Faye Brightmore (10)

Always

Yesterday you loved me,
Yesterday you cared,
Yesterday you realised the feelings we shared,
Today you still love me,
I'm still in your heart,
But today you know we are growing apart,
Tomorrow you'll hate me,
You'll forget the times we share,
Tomorrow my darling you won't be there,
Always I'll love you,
And always I'll care,
Always remember my darling,
Always, I'm there.

Micheala Chan (12)

This Person Is My Favourite

I read her books, I enjoy them very much,
It takes me to my story hutch,
Her books are excellent, they're a pleasure to read,
My imagination has grown just from a little tiny seed.
I hear every one of her fingers are full of rings,
But I bet each one of them diamond blings!
She has inspired me to be a writer,
I'm going to work very hard and never give up just like a fighter!
My dream is to become worldwide like her,
I just hope that dream will occur.
This person is my favourite not because of her looks,
But this person is my favourite because of her brilliant books.
This person is my favourite because she writes from the heart,
I know that her and her writing will never part.
This person is my favourite because of their amazing imagination,
This person has always been my inspiration.
Have you guessed my person yet?
Jacqueline Wilson is the best favourite person you can ever get!

Monique Jose (11)

My Favourite Person

I love my mum,
She's lots of fun,
She helps me all the time.
Mum cooks and cleans
Till everything gleams,
From morning until night.

And when I'm sad
Mum says, 'Things aren't so bad,'
With a kiss and a hug.
I'm as snug as a bug in a rug.
Mum's always there,
Mum always cares.
My mum - my *favourite* person!

Darcie Lonsdale (9)

My Mum

She's a white, drooping leather sofa, always sleeping,
She's a sweet yellow nightingale, always singing,
She's a burning, exploding fizzy drink in the hot sun,
She's a flaming marshmallow on the roasting evening fire.

She's as short as a newborn foal,
She's a perfume smelling of a rose,
She's a talking, colourful parrot making a nuisance,
She's a pink flower in the warm, blooming garden,
She's a young, soft, ginger kitten purring for her food.

She's a wobbly, shaky writer,
She's as hot as a lighter,
She never gives in,
She's as hard as tin,
She's got a smile on her face,
Stuck up like lace,
Ask anybody, there is no one like
My mum!

Safoorah Dhalech (10)

My Dublin And Derry Buddies

My Dublin buddy Lorraine is insane,
She makes me laugh and tiggles me till I cry!
She is the sparkle in the sky!
She sings aloud and dances on the clouds!
She listens, shouts and gives out
But she is the best buddy without a doubt!

My Derry buddy Evelyn is a scream!
She is the baking queen,
Fairy cakes, sponge cakes, cheesecakes, chocolate cakes!
You name it, she bakes it!
We bake, we laugh, we clean, we walk, we dream!
She is the sugar in the cream!
Me and my buddies, the dream team!

Caitlin Doherty (8)

Barney The Dog

He may be loopy
He may be lively
Call him what you like
Say he's mad
I won't care
'Cause he's the best
As far as I'm concerned.

He may escape
He may wreck the house
He doesn't care
He'll do anything
As long as it's something.

He may be barmy
He's still our Barney
He may be mad
But we don't care
Dogs are lovely anywhere!

Lucy Chandler (10)

My Mum

Fun as a Ferris wheel,
Comforting as a cat,
My favourite person is even better than that.

She is happy and joyful,
Exciting and cool,
And when she smiles, she lights up the room.

When I come home from school
She is always there,
Ready to listen and be fair.

My favourite person is very special to me,
For she is not just a friend . . .
But my mum, you see!

Rebecca Webster (11)

My Favourite People

M any people I do love,
Y et only one cannot get the shove,

F ather, because he owns a cool car,
A nd Mother because she makes jam in jars;
V ery many friends from way afar
O ther people, like my aunts, and
U ncles too, who want and want.
R eading books I love my sister Phoebe for,
I t's Aidan who loves daring things, cool!
' T is never enough to have favourite people,
E veryone is special to you!

P ersephone, my little sister
E ver goes out, I always miss her,
O h so many people, it's hard to choose,
P eople come and go, I get so confused!
L ike to say that is my best friend Maddie,
E ach one is special, but mine is my . . . Daddy!

Lorelei Makepeace Nielsen (11)

My Brother

He's annoying, he's fun
He's a pain in the bum
He's Alex.

His favourite colour's green
He is supreme
He's Alex.

He loves to mess about
He loves to shout
He's Alex.

He's my brother
I don't want another
He's mine, he's Alex!

James Burnham (9)

My Favourite Person

M y friend is so nice
Y ou're always there for me

F riends are true and faithful
A nd they're always there for you
V ery caring is what they are
O ur friendship will always last
U nder the sun we play together
R unning through the grass
I 'll always be here for you
T ime will never run out
E lizabeth is your name

P eople say we are like sisters
E veryone knows so well
R eally, really well
S uperstar is our nickname
O ur families can always tell
N o one will ever be as good as you.

Rachael Forsythe (10)

Mishka My Cat

Mishka, Mishka, fur and whiskers,
Playing in the backyard.
Down came a fly and hit her in the eye
Oh poor, poor Mishka.
Down comes a bee and stings her little knee
Miaow, miaow, miaow.
When she went to sleep she had a sneaky peep
To see if they came back.
When she wakes she will get them back
As she loves to eat them flies, *yum-yum!*
She licks her paws and cleans her mouth
And with a yawn she drops back off thinking what she can do next.
Watch out spiders!

Charlie Mills (10)

My Nan

My favourite person is my nan
I am a great big fan
She tells me things
That will help me win
Also makes me laugh.

My favourite person is my nan
I am a great big fan
She is like a teacher
With a beautiful feature
Also makes me laugh.

My favourite person is my nan
I am a great big fan
She cooks roast on a Sunday
Not on a Monday
It's very tasty
She is definitely not hasty
Also makes me laugh.

Layla Moghaddam (10)

My Favourite Person

My favourite person loves doing art
Now goes to college
Her name is Leanne and she is my sister
My favourite person I love so much
She loves me too
My favourite person loves doing art
Now goes to college
She's very pretty
She's great at singing
My favourite person
Now goes to college
She doesn't live with me
And I miss her a lot.

Niamh Woods (8)

My Favourite Cousin

M y cousin is my best friend,
Y ears of love which will never end.

F ame and fortune is her dream,
A nd outstanding grades to be seen,
V aluable and precious in my heart,
O ur love will never be apart,
U nderstanding and very sociable,
R esponsible but sometimes emotional,
I ncredible amount of love she has,
T ogether with fun and pizzazz,
E very day I miss her razzmatazz!

C aring for me through the years,
O ur love has grown with laughter and tears,
U nique ambitions she has for the future,
S tudying harder and harder to become a teacher,
I nventive and creative is her mind,
N oticeably gorgeous and always kind.

Aisha Kayani (11)

My Favourite Person?

The person I have picked is Lizzy.
Lizzy is a busy person but always has a smile.
If you are feeling down, then Lizzy is the one,
She will always be the one,
Even if you think you can't find a smile.
If one day I can't find anything to wear
Then I'll call Lizzy.
She'll always have something there.
If you can't do something important,
Then ask Lizzy,
She is always a helping hand.
Last but not least,
Lizzy is a double-bubble person.

Emily-Jane Bayliss (10)

My Favourite Person

My favourite person is my mummy,
She gives me hugs and she's very funny,

My favourite person is my daddy,
He loves playing golf but he doesn't have a caddy

My favourite person is my sister,
She loves running; she's got lots of blisters

My favourite person is my friend Alice,
One day I think she's going to own a palace

My favourite person is my neighbour Anne,
She's always around to lend us a hand

My favourite person is my teacher,
I put a whoopee cushion under her chair,
Ha that will teach ya!

My last favourite person is our school helper, Sam,
Alice is her daughter and she is her mam.

Erin Seabrook (10)

You Are My Secret (You Are My Favourite Secret)

Your green eyes are like two jewels of jade.
Your skin can be compared to the snow in the winter's fall.
Your laugh is a symphony in an orchestra band,
Every move you make is as elegant as a ballet dancer,
Your smile is the sun in the sky,
Something good, something right,
Something made by the glory and power itself
This person is my hero, this person is my friend
This person is a secret so my lips are sealed
This person is for me myself and I am an angel in Heaven's sky.
But really and truly the angel sits right next to me every day of my life.

Fiona Chaitezvi (11)

Beyond The Mirror

She has soft brown eyes
And silky black hair.
The tone of her face,
Her skin glows, she is so fair.

She is very friendly,
Always smiles.
She is lovable
And cares about the latest styles.

She likes to party,
And read magazines,
Going out with friends
She is such a queen.

It is hard for me to part with her
As we are so close.
When I put the mirror down
She is gone, I miss her the most.

Zainah Muddassir (11)

Untitled

As I walk down the hall full of cold and dark
At the very end, I see a small spark

It's as light as the stars in a pitch-black sky
Amazed by the brightness as I walk on by

As I stand thinking of the star I see
I hear you all ask, what could it be?

For this star is such a beautiful thing
But not just a thing, a human being

This dazzling light has been here for years
Through my darkest hours and my deepest fears

See this person you say you must see
She is my mother, the mother of me.

Samuel Howell (11)

My Friend, My Dog

He follows me around the house
With various things to play with
And races me to the top of the stairs
Wrestling all the way up.

At tea he is focused on me
He knows I'm weak
His pointed ears, his glassy stare
He does this every week.

He gets me into trouble
Eats biscuits off the plate
I have to take the rap for this
He'd do the same for me.

We bounce about together
Rogues on legs are we
The world would be our oyster
But he'd eat it in front of me.

Adam Bell (9)

A Loving Mother

A mother's love lasts forever
It never goes away altogether
My mother bought me my first lovely toy
She always fills my heart with joy
My mum fills my life with love
And she is like the stars from high above
We always care for each other
I really love my mother
My mum is like the silver moon at night
Because they both shine very bright
My mother is more precious than a mountain of gold
And I should always do as I'm told
My wonderful mother is the best
Far better than the rest.

Fatimah Mohd-Fauzi (8)

That Special Someone I Call My Brother

My brother is very special to me
He helps me through a lot
He's always there when I need him
A true friend of a brother's what I've got.

From the times that we have argued
We made up and started again
I don't know what I'd do without him
When he's gone what will I do then?

It's not easy to say sorry
But he makes me realise
That it makes people feel better
When you do apologise.

I don't know how lucky I am
To have such a caring brother like mine
There for me every day
And looking out for me all the time.

Marissa Patel (11)

Mum

My mum is not like any other mum,
My mum is the best mum in the world.
Some kids say, 'Mum, you're the best mum in the world,'
But I know that's not true,
Because when I shout it from the rooftops,
I know that I love you, and that is true.
Your hug is warm and comforting
And you smell like morning dew.
Your eyes sparkle like stars on a clear night
And your teeth are as white as the moon.
Your eyes area as green as a tiny blade of grass
On a misty morning,
And these are all the reasons
Why I love you all the more.

David Swan (11)

What Would I Be Without You?

Where do I start?
She's such a sweetheart
She's lively, cheerful and vibrant
Jaunty, upbeat and buoyant.

She's so jokey and loveable
Benevolent and thoughtful
You could never stay angry at her for long
She'll win you over with a game or a song.

When I'm ill or feeling down
She'll be at my side without a frown
Her sweet smile lights up her face
And comforts me like the warmth of her embrace.

When I'm old and grey
And my favourite person is far away
My mum is my favourite and much more
She's the best person I will ever adore.

Shivani Nathu (12)

My Best Mate

My best friend is Millie Moo,
Long and thin with a wiry tail.
A sausage dog can't you tell,
A chocolate apple dapple and fluffy too.
She's with me wherever I am too.
She's small and neat and very sweet.
When I go to bed she lies by my feet
She cheers me up when I'm upset.
This is what makes Millie my favourite pet.
If she gets poorly it's me that takes her to the vets.
She looks at me with a sparkle in her eye,
Then I know she's gonna run around the room like a crazy baboon.
Me and Millie are both very silly
Always together and faithful forever.

Isobel Sword (10)

My Dad

My favourite person is my dad
He is always there for me
He lifts my mood up when I am sad
And we both love to go to the sea.

Me and my dad like the same things
We make a great team together
We both like to eat chicken wings
And we will be father and son forever.

Me and my dad both love France
And we like to travel a lot
And we also like to dance
But when we start we can never stop.

Me and my dad have a special bond
And our bond will never end
But this is how we belong
He is not just my dad, he is my friend!

Osragli Elezi (11)

My Favourite Person

My favourite person is Lilly Ray,
She plays with me all day
And when we meet each other any day
We both say hi or hey.
But one day our mums said
Lilly Ray could sleep over,
So we went to a restaurant
Called Buckingham Lay,
Then we went home and we
Played and ate our meal.
After, we played, then the time
Had come to go to bed,
So before we went to bed we said,
'Goodnight, sleep tight.'

Esraa Fahmy (8)

My Best Friend Annie

My favourite person is Annie
She's my very best friend
We talk to each other on MSN
And she always has something to send.

She has a sister, Daisy,
And a brother, Jack.
They all go to athletics,
Down at the running track.

I went round for a sleepover,
A couple of weeks ago.
We both had a fantastic time,
Until I had to go.

Annie's really funny,
She's acts just like a clown,
She really is the best friend,
In the whole of Kettering town.

Holly Chambers (10)

Who's My Favourite Teacher?

Mr Hardcastle or Mrs Patel?
I don't think I should tell
Mr Farrar or Mrs Clark?
As we sing in assembly, singing like a lark
Mr Evans or Mrs T
Or Mrs Neal who's crazy about a wasp or a bee?
School's out
Before I go out and about
I think I should tell
Mrs T!
You're the one for me!
Blonde and blue-eyed.
Hope I don't get detention
For this teacher's mention!

Sophie Hall (10)

My Friend, Tim

Tim waits for me each morning
Behind the garden shed,
He has masses of golden hair and ghostly white skin . . .
He's always there, my friend Tim.

Tim walks me to school each morning
And drops me by the gate,
I turn around as he waves goodbye,
He's always there, my friend Tim.

I wait longingly for 3 o'clock
And watch the hours slowly tick by.
I dash out of school, straight to the gate,
He's always there, my friend Tim.

The best thing about having a pretend friend is . . .
They're always there for you.
I smile at him as he disappears to his shed.
He'll be back again, my friend Tim!

Bethany Cook (11)

Michael Jackson

My favourite person was
One of the greatest singers
The world had ever met.
Every time I listen to one of his songs
I feel like I am on stage performing with him.
He was
An inspiration to others,
A perfect role model,
Someone I admired.
Sometimes he was in the press for the wrong things,
But no one is perfect.
Some people call him the King of Pop,
Others call him a hero.
I just call him Michael Jackson.

Kirran Khan (12)

My Uncle Jamie

I have a lot of family
Of which I'm very fond
This person in particular
Is tall and very blond.

When he comes to see me
He really is a scream
He always makes me giggle
When he's on my trampoline.

He likes to sing to music
Which is always very loud
He dresses cool and stylish
And he stands out in a crowd.

He is a fashion expert
That's what I would like to be
As super-hip and trendy
Like my Uncle Jamie.

Ellie Barnfield (10)

My Favourite Person

My favourite person has thick brown hair,
If only she'd clean it!
My favourite person has a lovely pink room,
If only she'd tidy it!
My favourite person has a golden retriever dog,
If only she'd walk it!
My favourite person has a black witch's cat,
If only she'd brush it!
My favourite person has lots of homework,
If only she'd do it!
My favourite person has lots of fun toys,
If only she'd use them!
My favourite person is the world's luckiest little girl.
My favourite person is *me!*

Niamh Lundy (11)

My Dad

My dad is cool
In a weird sort of way
He acts like a fool
And lays around some of the day.

His hair is grey
But I love him anyway
He takes us places
And pulls funny faces.

He does the shopping
For all the food we can eat
He Hoovers and cleans
To make our house tidy and neat.

My dad is cool
He's so unique
He's got that special touch
That's why I love him so very, very much.

Cassie Devereux (10)

My Mum

My mum, well what shall I say?
My mum is very pretty and has beautiful eyes,
My mum looks wonderful in Punjabi suits and in English clothes.
That's why my mum has very good colour combination!
And to tell you the truth, my mum is very wise!
My mum is very lovely and she is very snugly,
She loves to exercise because she wants to be fit and healthy,
And that's why my mum is very energetic,
She loves to work hard and dance.
I have to say that my mum is a bit strict when we do not listen.
My mum always makes sure I do well in school and out of school!
She helps us around the house when we need help,
And takes us out everywhere!
I am very proud to be called her daughter!

Teerith Sehmi (12)

My Auntie

All the intricate patterns
It makes me want to stare
Her nails look like a beauty
I can't believe they were once bare.

Her nails sparkle in the sun
With flowers on and hearts
I wonder how she does it
The question's tearing me apart.

Her colour choice is wonderful
The beads she uses are very cool
It's as beautiful as a waterfall
But that's not all.

Everything she creates
Turns out to be a masterpiece
She's loving and caring
And I'm proud to be her niece.

Ella Rayment (10)

My Mum

My mum brightens up my day
In every single way!
Always changing my sister's nappies,
She always finds a way to make me happy.
Also keeping my room neat,
She still has time to give me something to eat.
If I had the choice, I'd give her 'Mum of the Year'
And for my room's sake I'd keep her near!
If I were to go against my greatest fear,
With my mum around I wouldn't shed a tear.
It sounds like my mum's got ten hands,
But I can tell you I'm her number one fan!
Cooking, cleaning and caring too,
I'd have this mum if I were you!

Tyler Poyner (11)

Jack (Sprat)

I have a little dog
He's like a teddy bear
He has a thick fur coat
And I tickle him under there.

He has a poky tongue
That sticks out in the air
When Jack Frost is around
It will no longer be there.

He loves his chocolate drops
At bedtime when he flops
He takes up half the bed
With his bum right next to my head.

I love my little dog
Of that I can't deny
If he should ever die
I'll have to say goodbye . . . goodbye!

Kain Hooper (11)

My Favourite Person

This girl is quite bright
Like the spark of a light
Her hair is shiny and gold
And it is hard for her mind to unfold
She can sometimes be lazy
But is definitely crazy
This girl has a musical flair
And likes to jump and dance high in the air
Her sparkling blue eyes
Are like the colour of the skies
It is strange why I chose
This person to be my favourite
Do you know why?
It's me!

Annabel Streete (11)

Untitled

My favourite person in the world
Is beautiful and fab,
Always entertaining people,
She's never, ever sad.

Loyal, positive, really cool,
Everybody's friend.
She wears the bestest clothes
To keep up with the trend.

A drama queen, a bossy-boots,
An actress in the making,
Hollywood's latest film star
Is hers for the taking!

Dancing is her thing,
Of course, everyone would agree.
I think I should tell you now,
My favourite person is *me!*

Georgia Woodley (11)

My Best Friend!

My best friend is Skye,
That's because she doesn't lie.
She will be my friend forever,
Forget her? No never.
There will be a special space,
In my head, that's her place.
Just because we're moving on,
Doesn't mean I can't see her,
We will meet up some time along,
The paths we choose to take.
Skye is so much fun,
A great friend to everyone.
I will miss her very much
But watch out, we'll meet up.

Charlotte Mills (11)

Can You Guess Who I Mean?

My favourite person is two feet tall,
He's blond and very cheeky,
Can you guess who I mean?
He's rather very sneaky!

His favourite programme is 'Auntie Mabel',
He watches it all day long,
Can you guess who I mean?
He's always singing the song!

He loves to go on the train
With Grandad and Nan Sue.
Can you guess who I mean?
I like trains too!

I haven't told you the person's name,
He's really quite a grub.
Can you guess who I mean?
It's my brother, Jacob!

Olivia Barker (11)

Funny Finlay

Finlay is so funny
In the water
Nobody could be so bright and sunny.
Finlay can laugh more than any other child.
He plays really good
And he does sometimes go wild.
Finlay eats hoops
They're really messy
But they taste good.
Once he licked a slug
And he watches a big red bus
That goes *chug, chug, chug.*
I love Mr Finbow Fin
Who is 3 years old.

Emily McGowan (9)

My Favourite Person, Misty

I have a favourite person
Who is very, very shy
She loves to snuggle on my lap
And let me tell you why

She's my tabby cat called Misty
She's very, very small
She likes to curl up on my lap
Because it's very warm

She loves to jump and play around
With her favourite ball
She chases it round the furniture
She chases it down the hall

She's been my favourite person
Since the day we brought her home
I can't imagine life without her
I'd be so alone.

Chloe Cox (10)

My Mum And Dad

My mum and dad are very sweet,
They give me food and lots to eat.
They tuck me up in bed at night
And keep me warm when it's cold outside.
Mums are very helpful, they do the washing up,
They make our bed and keep us clean and buy us lots of stuff
Dads are very thoughtful, they do their job just right,
But when they take us out on outings we just say, 'Alright!'
They buy us lots of things and think of us as lightning,
Is that truly what we are or are we a little frightening?
Brothers are very naughty, they beat us a lot,
They think of us as punch bags and use us quite a lot.
But overall that doesn't mean that they don't love us so,
They love us very much but they find it hard to show!

Sophie Woolnough (10)

My Favourite Person

My favourite person
Makes me smile
My favourite person
Has a lot of style

My favourite person
Cheers me up
My favourite person
Wishes me luck

My favourite person
Is always sharing
My favourite person
Is very caring

My favourite person
Loves me a lot
My favourite person
Is the best friend I've got.

Eloise Hadley (10)

My Favourite Person

My favourite person is my mum,
We do activities together, they are such fun.
She likes to cook my favourite food
And always puts me in a happy mood.
Me and my mum we share beauty tips,
We love going on shopping trips.
We hug and kiss each other every day,
To make us feel special in every way.
She helps me with my homework, giving advice,
I really love my mum, she is really nice.
She knows my favourite toys are Dr Who,
She likes to surprise me, that's what she'll do.
My mum helps me choose the clothes I wear,
I adore my mum, she is always there.

Jade Thompson (11)

My Favourite Person

Everyone's got a favourite person
We all have one that's unique
Mine is my best friend, Ebony
She's small, dark, friendly and sleek.

Ebony will always listen to you
She'll never interrupt saying, 'What? Why?'
She doesn't get upset or frustrated
Ebony is also very honest and won't lie.

Ebony is extremely intelligent
She always knows when I'm sad
She will come and give me a cuddle
And help me see life's not so bad.

My favourite person is different
She likes to stretch and purr
My favourite person is my cat, Ebony
And I will always love her.

Holly Young (11)

My Sister

My sister is mine, my sister is fin
My sister might grind her teeth and suck her thumb
But most of all she loves my mum

My sister is my mate, my sister is so great
She is very small and I'm very tall
She can't even throw a ball
But I can do it all

She cries a lot, especially when she's hot
But Mum is the only one that can make her stop
But I still think she's top of the top
She is never happy when she's in a dirty nappy
But Mum's the only one who changes her
Never my daddy!

Mariyah Wolfenden (10)

My Grandad And Me

My grandad makes me laugh
When he tells his jokes
He makes everyone laugh
Even all the old folks

My grandad will always
Laugh and cheer
He will definitely win
Best Grandad of the year

We have so much fun
Doing what we do best
Getting messy and mucky
And all of the rest

I jump up and down
And shout, 'Yippee,'
Cos today it'll be
My grandad and me.

Ellie Kate Trafford (10)

My Granny

She is so keen and I don't know how she does it
A busy bee, an early riser
Briskly swimming in the early morning
I don't know anyone like her

Unstoppable she flies on her bike
She takes to anything like a duck to water
Living life how it comes
Once her fingers start to get working
The magic begins, it flows through her body
Beautiful smells of cooking waft gently

She will hug me close and delight at my successes
Granny of ten and my granny too
Wherever you are this poem's for you.

Esther Darling (10)

Young Writers

My Hamster

His name is Donut,
And I'll tell you what,
He's my hamster,
I love him a lot!

He runs all night,
He sleeps all day,
He has some fun
When he wants to play.

All the time
He's getting fat,
He eats all day,
I'll tell you that!

I clean his cage
Every week,
He loves his wheel,
But it does squeak!

Rebecca Andrew (10)

My Mum

You're the thousand stars that light the darkest nights,
You're the peace and happiness that stops the war and fight,
You are like an eagle; so strong and wise,
Your love and happiness for me is something that never dies.

You're the thousand secrets that blow,
You're the first drop of snow,
You're the queen of the land,
You're like the shiniest piece of sand,
You're like the moon that shines and glows,
You're the streams and rivers that flow.

You're special to me,
I'm sure you'd agree,
Because my role model's my mum.

Muna Elayeh (11)

My Mom's Great Super Powers

My mom has great super powers
She can wash the dishes while having a shower
She can balance 10 CDs on top of her head
And write a long story while she is in bed.

My mom has great super powers
She can ride a horse while building a tower
She can tidy the house in one great sweep
And bake a cake while she is asleep.

My mom has great super powers
She can make a feast in just one hour
She can paint a winning portrait with just one hand
And draw a submarine in the soft, golden sand.

My mom has great super powers
She could lay all day in a big field of flowers
She could wander into the bright moonlight
And disappear into the great, starry night.

Sophie Cox (11)

My Baby Brother

He was born in May,
For me and my family it was a very special day,
I enjoyed watching him growing,
But I hate him jumping on my bed every morning.

He is one year old,
It is very funny when he shaves his head bald
He enjoys dancing to music,
He entertains us all,
When he gets tired he suddenly starts to fall.

He is still very small,
But he has begun to walk,
We wish him all the best,
For the day he begins to talk.

Sohail Ahmed (11)

My Furry Friend, Toffee

My rabbit's named Toffee,
Se's the colour of coffee,
Runs like lightning
And finds aeroplanes frightening.

Her ears are very floppy
Because her breed is a mini loppy.
She runs around all day
And loves to play.

She loves to sit in a ball
So round, cute and small,
And follows me round the house
As quiet as a mouse.

She is terrified of the rain
And finds her sister, Peaches, a pain.
I wish you could meet my rabbit, Toffee,
The colour of coffee.

Ruby Gill (10)

My Best Friend

We hang at the shops
Or at the park
We're always seen together
We split up just before dark.

She's like my other half
We're always on the phone
Running up the bill
(We are quite known).

We see each other every day
We are like sisters
Inseparable till the end
She went away for a day
And I missed her.

Natasha Baugh (11)

My Favourite People

My favourite people are my family
Well, sometimes
Who can blame me?

My brother and I argue
Over something like gloopy stew
He says, 'Yummy,' and I say, 'Eww!'

Sometimes Mum and Dad shout at me
Cos I won't eat my tea
Then Dad (who's no better than me)
Goes to watch Wayne Rooney
And Mum goes to do something arty.

But other times when Dad goes to town
I should give him a crown
Cos when he comes back
What do I see?
Lots and lots of delicious sweeties.

Rhiannon Gilbey (9)

My Friend Lilly

M y friend Lilly makes up funny words
Y ellow is one of her favourite colours

F riends are good but my friend Lilly's the best
R abbits come in her garden and nibble the grass
I ndia, her cheeky sister, keeps her on her toes
E ndless friendship between me and Lilly
N othing can stop us being friends
D reams to be Sharpay from High School Musical

L oving and caring to everyone
I n her Wendy house we colour and paint
L oopy Lilly has loopy hair
L illy can be very silly
Y ou're my best friend Lilly.

Prakriti Arora (7)

My Grandad

He is footie mad
It can't be bad
He supports Leeds
Which meets his needs.

My grandad is my favourite person.

He is funny
And he likes eating honey
He buys me ice cream
So that I don't *scream*.

My grandad is my favourite person.

My grandad is great
He is my mate
I can talk to him about anything
He is my everything.

I couldn't live without my grandad!

Keira Chew (10)

My Favourite Person

Harley, my dog,
Nine years old nearly
My mate, my buddy
My companion
Harley, my Staffordshire Bull Terrier.

Harley, my dog,
People think he is vicious
But he is precious
To me!

Harley, my dog,
Half-white, half-black
But full with love!

Harley, my dog, I love him so much!

Storm Rose (10)

My Favourite Person

My favourite person is as sweet
As a freshly-baked cake
Covered in glistening icing and sparkling sprinkles.

My favourite person is charming,
Smiling from cheek to cheek,
Always with a kind word,
Like a splash of sunshine on a rainy, stormy day.

My favourite person is generous,
Giving their time and donations to those in need.

My favourite person is considerate,
Giving their seat to an elderly person.

My favourite person is an inspiration to me,
By all the things they do and say,
Helps me want to be a better person day by day.

Can you guess who it is?

Eleanor Cunningham (10)

My Invisible Best Friend

When I wake up I think of you
When I close my eyes you're the face I see
When I dream, I dream of you and the best that we can be

My best friend from among the stars
From the far off depths of imagination
You and I are dreamers, our heads are in the clouds

My inspiration and my courage
We will carry on side by side
What I do, we do together, we can get through all

You are the best friend I could ever wish for
A perfect match, destined were we
It's a shame, my dear friend, you're invisible
My friend who's imaginary.

Kate Horwell (13)

My Favourite Person, Max

My favourite person has chocolate-brown fur,
He has a Basil Brush-like tail.
He has energetic, playful legs
And he loves to play ball.
I love him to bits.
But sadly he has fits.
About two years ago
He was diagnosed with epilepsy.
He has a wet, warm tongue,
He wouldn't hurt a fly,
But last year he accidentally
Caught my dad in the eye.
Don't worry, he's not blind!
He loves it when I'm rubbing his belly,
Usually when I'm watching the telly.
You are one in a million.
I love you, my Maximilian.

Jordi Morgan (12)

My Best Friend

Our secrets are whispered, our secrets are told
Our secrets are kept from the young and the old
She's my best friend and we never fight
She tells me her secrets and I hold them in tight.

Our dreams are whispered, our dreams are told
Our dreams are kept from the young and the old
She's my best friend and we never fight
I tell her my dreams and she holds them in tight.

She's my best friend, I love her loads
But sometimes we travel down bumpy roads
She's always there, she never leaves
She's always trusted and believes in me.

That's why she's my best friend, Freyja.

Megan Delaney (11)

My Favourite Person

When I'm hurt and I'm in pain
When I'm let down by the rain
I will look up to the sky
I'll say why oh why
Then something from a misty view
It was strange but it was true
Walked ahead and said to me
'I will fill your day with glee'
It was not an 'it' nor a 'he'
It was in fact a pretty she
It was in fact my cousin Leah
To me she's pretty and she's dear
She's kind, loving, sweet and caring
She's always giving, always sharing
We have so much fun when we play
She makes the sunshine last all day
Friends forever is what we say.

Maisy Syratt (8)

My Nan

One of my favourite people is my nan
And I will tell you why
Because she makes a smashing apple pie.

She was born on the 11th of July,
What a special day,
Most people agree so do I.

She is kind, caring, funny and sweet
And did I mention she is kinda neat?

She has seven grandchildren including me,
And I am certain she knows what she means to me.

There is nothing wrong with my nan you can see
The only thing I can think of, she is too kind to me!

Charlie Hall (11)

Furry Friend

My favourite person is George
He's black and very furry.
He's always there to greet me
When I go round to Gran's,
With woofs and barks and wagging tail,
He's always pleased to see me.
I always have a treat to spare
When we go for a walk,
He likes to have his tummy rubbed
And chew his tennis ball.
I wish that he could speak to me
So I know what he is thinking.
He's the leader of his gang and everybody loves him
For he's a gentle giant and really lovely.
He's the bestest friend I've ever had and I know he loves me back.
Have you guessed what George is?
Yes, he is a dog.

Ellis Anderson (10)

My Favourite Person Is My Mum

She has loved me since I was the size of her thumb,
She always knows my favourite sweets
And often buys me lots of treats.
She's constantly looking after me,
With special parties for us three.
Hugs and kisses after school,
Lots of fun in the swimming pool.
She always makes sure that I am fed
And when I'm ill I say, 'Can I get in your bed?'
Our holidays are full of joy and laughter
And I will remember them forever after.
I know that she will forever love me
And together always we will be.

Pia Joyce (8)

My Eccentric Nan

My eccentric nan is the most
Crazy person you will ever meet!
She's always buying and cooking me treats.
She can't help dancing and wiggling her feet!
My nan is a writer too,
She writes poems, songs and stories too!
She tells me of fairies, pixies and gnomes
Hiding in her secret garden,
Whether she's telling the truth, no one knows.
She can also talk to animals,
She tells me what they say.
She says her dog, Bobby,
Has an awful lot to say!
My nan is a joker, a comedienne, you could say!
She's always laughing and happy all day!
My nan is my favourite person for all the reasons I said,
Despite her mad and crazy head!

Alana Emms (11)

Gentle Cheryl

A young woman from Newcastle town
Came down to London to face the crowd
She sang and she danced and made her family proud
And became a member of Girls Aloud.

The young woman she grew and got lots of fame
She married a footballer and got in trouble, what a shame
She became a judge and everyone backed her
She became the queen of the X Factor.

Cheryl is by far my favourite star
She lights up my screen, I watch from afar
She is kind to the people who sing to the crowd
I wish I was with her in Girls Aloud.

Leila Charteris (10)

My Favourite Person For Always

My favourite person is my best friend,
Our friendship will never end.
We always have so much fun,
When I am alone I wish she would come.
Drawing and chatting,
Lots of laughing.

We are always together,
Friends forever,
Doing our secret handshake
And sharing each other's birthday cakes.
When one of us is sad,
We try to make each other glad.

All the great times we have had,
I am oh so glad
That we are best friends.
Our friendship will never end.

Emily Wong (11)

My Life-Changing Uncle And Me

All uncles are the same
Some have taken fame
All we can do is love them
And never take advantage of them.

Everyone's uncle is great deep down
Just turn around and your heart will pound
With how great they really are.

My uncle is the light in my life
He makes me enjoy every second of every night
He and I will hold onto each other like mould
He is one of those people who will never give up
Even if he had to tear through never-ending steel walls.

Isla Hoad (11)

Winston Is My Doggy, Winston Is My Friend

Winston is a big brown bear
And he dribbles everywhere.
He eats my daddy's walls
And never comes when we call.
He loves to eat
Anything from food
To rubbish off the street!

Winston has springs in his paws
Which he uses to jump up the doors.
When he gets brushed,
He has to be pushed
To stand still at all!

Winston is big, heavy and brown,
But he is like a light-footed clown!

Emma Batchelor (10)

My Best Friend

She's my best friend
My best friend forever
We spend nearly every day together.

We're honest to each other
And we are a team,
The perfect one as it may seem.

She helps me with a lot of things
And then I will help her,
To make life more enjoyable and a bit easier.

So basically,
She's right for me
And she always will be.

Her name is Emily.

Chloe O'Hara (10)

Grandma

Grandma; on her allotment digging the soil,
Planting the seeds, watering the greenhouse.
She's baking now!

Grandma; stirring the soup, mixing the flour,
Making jelly, yummy food!
She's tired now!

Grandma; lying on the sofa, doing the crossword,
Looks like you're sleeping or just resting your eyes?
She's up now!

Grandma; off to London, we hopped on the train,
We got to the museum and Ancient Egyptians were great!
Time to go now!

Grandma; always there supporting me, teaching me
And loving me.
My best friend now!

Anna McKay (9)

My Best Buddy

In all my days I've loved to play,
But one thing I kept inside.
My friend, my buddy, my mind and soul
I cannot push him aside.

My best friend is all I need.
If I'd been left alone
I'd build a dome and pick up the phone
'Cause buddies can live alone!

My favourite person can now be revealed
After giving you so many clues
My favourite person, my buddy, my pal is . . .
It's true!

Sasha Antoine (10)

What Is A Mother?

A mother is a person who shows you affection,
Who loves you through thick and thin,
And will do anything to see you smile.

Mothers will always make you feel proud,
And will buy you anything you want,
Mothers will encourage you to do your best,
Plus a mother will always love you.

Always keep these things in your head,
And your mother's back
For you never know when you'll need them,
So keep them close.

So ask yourself
Does your mother do all these things?
I bet you the answer is yes!

That is what a mother is to me!

Lakhraj Dhiman (11)

My Friend Michael

My friend, Michael, is born to write,
His nimble fingers work all night.
They tell of unicorns, lions and sand giants so tall,
Horses, people and armies behind wire walls.

When I crawl into bed
I pick up his books and they take away all of the dread
Of the rainy morning I'll wake up to,
And all the chores I'll have to do.

My friends laugh at me for loving him so much,
And cherishing the books that I read and touch,
But Michael Morpurgo is the best author in the world,
And every time I read his books they help me unfurl.

Daisy Ellis (10)

My Favourite Person

My mum is so great
She won't shout if I'm late

My mum cooks me food
But she'll shout if I'm rude

Hurry, hurry back inside
Just before dinnertime

My mum likes me a lot
She gives me suncream when it's hot

My mum calls me in
When it's time to eat chicken

Hurry, hurry back inside
Just before dinnertime

This poem is about my mum
She always tells me to wipe my bum.

Waqas Arshad (11)

Mrs Lee

You have helped me for four long years,
When I was being bullied I had so many tears.
I used to hate reading, preferring to play,
But now I love reading every day.
My class didn't understand me, I felt really bad,
Things changed with the 'Chameleon Group', I'm no longer sad.

I think you're like a diary, always on 'Team Will',
With you all my difficulties came to a standstill.
Now my confidence has grown, I'll be anything I want to be,
Now everyone in my class really likes me.
Yes I'm dyslexic, but I can dance, sing and act,
I'm also clever and funny, and that's a fact.

You have been with me right to the end,
Mrs Lee, you're not just my teacher, you're also my friend.

Will Bourn (10)

My Best Friend Taylor

I've got a friend called Taylor
Who would like to run for mayor

Taylor is so funny
She is cute as a bunny

I'm a little bit tall
But she is so small

I love all animals
But she only likes mammals

We like to play
Outside on a summer's day

We like to make a big bang
Also we like to chill and hang

Taylor is the best
Actually she is better than the rest.

Bethany Halley (10)

My Favourite Person

My favourite person
Is a person who
Will understand me
Help me, support me
Never ever use me

He has to be friendly
He has to be fun
He has to be generous
And we will stay friends

Now on to me
If I met this person
On my way
I will respect him
And stay his best mate.

Domantas Stankus (9)

My Favourite Person

When I was honoured with this quest,
I thought of the person I liked best.

Celebrities, idols, popped into my mind
But then it hit me, how was I so blind?

My favourite brought guidance and love,
And the word of Islam from above.

Muhammed (PBUH) was His blessed name,
He taught peace and harmony when He came.

He was a man who led a truthful life,
Who guided mankind through all the strife,

And in the process suffered much,
But He never lost His special touch.

For all those reasons He is remembered today,
His memory is cherished and will never fade away.

Isra Dar (12)

Sox, My Little Pussycat

I have a little pussycat, his name is Sox
At the age of 14 weeks is as strong as an ox
He's black and white
And likes to bite
He is one of my favourite things.

I have a little pussycat, his name is Sox
He hunts like a fox
And sleeps in a box
He is one of my favourite things.

I have a little pussycat, his name is Sox
He chases things that go tick-tock
He jumps mega high
And touches the sky
Sox is one of my favourite things.

Ethan Cleary (11)

My Best Friend

I have lots of really good friends
We play, text and phone until the day ends
We ride our bikes and swim in the pool
Or hang out and listen to music which is cool
Sometimes we jump on my trampoline
Just on occasions we're quarrelsome and mean
But we always make up by the end of the day
And arrange to meet soon, a new game to play.

But when I'm sad or worried or down
I don't run away or take a bus to town
When I need to talk or moan or complain
I don't want to leave by boat or train
I just need someone I really trust
Someone to listen, advise and not fuss
To be my best friend so that I am not glum
There's always one person I turn to, my mum.

Grace Robertson (9)

Memories

Your eyes are always smiling
Your face lights up the room
You always make me smile
When I feel a little gloom
You never cease to fail me
When I need a little hug
You'd come into my bedroom
And we'd have a little snug
I wish you were still with me
And not so far away
It's not the same when I go out
And you're not there to play
You were the best dog that I ever had
And just saying your name again,
'Fallon,' makes me a little sad.

Conah Casson-Suratan (11)

My Favourite Person

Throughout the summer holidays,
My favourite person would have to be
The lovely, funny, kind Lisa
Who works on D33.

When I'm having treatment
And I'm feel scared and alone,
We will get Where's Wally?
Find him, his dog and bone.

If I'm bored as I'm having my IVs
She'll find games, crafts, puzzles
And plenty of DVDs.

Even though I have to spend time in hospital,
I don't feel glum.
I know Lisa will always be there,
And she's fun, fun, fun . . .

Jade Palmer (9)

My Favourite Person Ben

My favourite person Ben
Is my furry, furry friend
He's brown and white
And sleeps all night
He plays with his toy
He's a very good boy!
And when he barks
I will take him to the park
We run and jump and fall
While chasing after the ball
He eats his food
This puts him in a good mood
He hides behind some logs
There he is, my favourite person,
'The dog!'

Samuel Vaughan (10)

110

My Friend, Scooby

He'll bask peacefully, completely at ease,
In slivers of radiant sun.
A torrent of comfort flows over him,
When you tickle his ear or tum!
He runs around tirelessly in fields of green,
Like an orange flame a-flare.
He sits on my mama's knee jubilantly like a king,
While my mama rests in her chair.
His cuddly fur is as soft as silk,
His tail's like a ginger whip.
He's got sharp claws, but he doesn't use them,
They could really use a clip!
Overall he's my favourite dog,
A great friend to me.
There could be no one better
Than my buddy, Scooby!

Joe Lidgett (11)

These People Are The Best

I don't have a favourite person,
I don't rate one above the rest,
But if I really had to choose,
These people are the best.
My mum's artistic, kind and caring,
My dad's a funny football fan,
My sister's a loving teenager,
But there are still more in my clan.
My aunt's a kind and sporty lady,
My other aunt is mad.
Yet another aunt's a school headmistress,
My two best friends are hyper,
Some might say insane!

These people I do rate above the rest.
These people are the best!

Roisin McKeegan (11)

My Favourite Nanny, Pam

My favourite person,
Now let me see,
So many people mean the world to me,
But my favourite, I have to say,
Is my nan,
My nanny, Pam.
She picks me up when I am down,
She makes me smile when I frown,
She makes me laugh when I cry,
We watch telly and play I Spy.
She tells me off when I am wrong,
We laze about all day long.
Now she is poorly, not getting better,
I just want to tell the world
Just how much I love her.
Love you, Nanny Pam.

Shannon Windle (12)

My Little Dog Jess

Jess is asleep on my bed,
Her little wet nose against my head,
Dreaming of all the things we have done,
Being together and having fun.

On Monday we went to London to visit the Queen.
On Tuesday we sat on the beach with ice cream.
On Wednesday we went for a walk round the lakes.
On Thursday we had a picnic with tea and cakes.
On Friday we went to the pet shop to buy some treats.
On Saturday it thundered and you hid under my sheets.
On Sunday we played all day, until it was time for bed.
Your little wet nose against my head,
I will miss you my little friend,
But be sure to always remember,
I will love you until the end.

Tasha Bull (11)

My Mum

Like a Roman candle we all stare in awe
She will come to rescue me and bring me back ashore
She tells me great stories of places she has been
And Hoovers the carpets so they'll be nice and clean
If I cry she will wipe the tears from my eyes
She is like an owl exceedingly clever and wise
As brave as a lion, but without the bite
She teaches me life lessons so I will do right
Buying me new clothes so I will stay cool
She's also a perfect taxi for taking me to school
Making cooked breakfast, dinner and tea
However busy she is, she always has time for me
When I've had a shower, she blow-dries my hair
When I'm eating chocolate, with her I will share
If I shout for help, she will always come
She'll always be my favourite because she's my mum.

Emily Davies (11)

Mum

A crystal-clear waterfall filled with individual jewels
Trickling down every rock it gushes past
Before plunging into a lagoon with turquoise tranquillity

A single raindrop glistening on a rose petal in the sunlight
Like a thousand diamonds joined into one
Giving off a gentle red glow

The creamiest chocolate melting in your mouth
A warm trickling chocolatey sensation
Running down the back of your throat
Each bite different from the one before and the one after

My mum
Totally different
Totally special
Totally mine.

Cait Stead (11)

My Favourite Person

My favourite person is Dylan Sprouse
He's great on TV, has an awesome house
Last year I met him on a Disney cruise
When we were talking, all he cared about were his shoes
He has a twin brother, his name is Cole
When I saw them both together it lifted my soul
My dream is to be an actress like Dylan and his twin
Maybe someday if I am lucky
I'll be just like him
Dylan's stage name is Zack
Short for Zachary
But it makes no difference what he's called
He's just wonderful to me
Dylan's funny, handsome and clever
I can't wait to watch him on TV
I think I'll love him forever.

Nadine Barber (11)

My Best Friend

Read this poem and draw what you read
You'll discover a person special to me

- B londe hair to the chin
- E yes as blue as the sky
- S miles as great as a dolphin
- T eeth whiter than white

- F antastic curls in her hair
- R osy cheeks
- I ncredible classmate
- E xcellent Irish dancer
- N ever gives up
- D oesn't need to pretend
    Because she's my *best friend*

Now you can see my best friend's called Betty!

Muna Abdelrahman (11)

Kara, Our Kind Cat

Kara, our family cat,
She curls up on our mat,
She's always sweet and caring
But not ever so daring.
We got her from a rescue home,
She came to our house and started to moan.
When she glanced at the fish in our tank,
We knew what was going to happen as the fish sank.
She hates to go outside,
Hoping to stay in and hide.
Her favourite place is my room.
If my dad finds out there will be a loud boom!
So here's my cat, Kara,
Who you find is very sneaky.
Luckily you don't have her
To wake up with your eyes tired and peaky.

Mia Critchley (11)

More Than A Mother

When God set the world in place
When He hung the stars up in space
When He made the land and the sea
Then He made you and me.

He sat back and saw all that was good
He saw things to be as they should
Just one more blessing He had in store
He created a mother, but whatever for?

He knew a mother would have a special place
To shine His reflection on her child's face
A mother will walk the extra mile
Just to see her children smile.

I'm glad to choose to be all this and more to me
You share a love that knows no end.

Asviny Arulanantham (9)

My Favourite Person

My favourite person is my dad
Because he never makes me sad
He is always a winner in chess
Plus he doesn't make such a mess
My dad will of course
Buy me a horse
He has adventures with me
And we go to the sea
He buys me what I want
He's always at the front
He came to help me when I fell on my knee
We love the taste of the honey from the bee
He gave me a flower
Which gave me power
We go swimming together
We will never break up, ever.

Asmaa Hafez (9)

My Lovely Mum

My lovely mum makes me feel warm and snugly
She is never too busy for a cuddle
I love my mum, she is so cool
She takes and picks me up from school
Fetching, carrying, cleaning, washing
Cooking, ironing, she does the lot
I love my mum, she is so great
That sometimes she lets me stay up late
My mum sees to most of my wishes
She also does the dirty dishes
My mum is fashion mad but football sad
A gold star carer but definitely not a chocolate sharer
You see my mum is the best in the world
And I would not swap her for a diamond or a pearl
My favourite person is my mum!

Milly Tye (9)

Lazy Uncle Andrew

L azy Uncle
A ndrew
Z zzzz half the day
Y awns

U p he gets
N ext has a shower
C old water
L ong time getting ready
E ats a bowl of cereal for breakfast

A nd then has lunch
N ext goes shopping
D oes buy clothes after
R uns home for supper then
E ats a bowl of cereal
W atches telly 'til late.

Amelia Mapson (9)

What Makes Me Smile

What makes me smile is one of my furry friends

He's there in the morning
He's there at night

He's there when I'm happy
He's there when I'm sad

He's there when I'm tired
He's there when I'm playful

He's there when I'm grumpy
He's there when I'm not

He's there when I'm playing
He's there when I'm bored

He's always there
It's my dog Harvey.

Chloe Glover (11)

My Favourite Animal

Spike is my cat
He's not thin or too fat
Sometimes he is playful and sometimes sleepy
He's as fluffy as a teddy bear
His coat is black and white.

He's always feeling hungry
He helps himself to treats
He purrs and rubs against me
When it's time for tea
And then he has a sleep.

He comes to bed
And rests himself above my head
In the morning he taps my face
Then he says miaow
Spike is my special cat.

Emma Jane Langhorn (11)

My Favourite Person

My dad's the best,
Better than the rest.
Strong like a rock,
Plays football like Messi,
Hardworking like a businessman
And has a heart of gold.
Just see how he walks, talks and laughs.
I know all dads are great,
But my dad's the best.
He gives me games and money,
He is my role model and
He is my best friend.
He gives me everything,
And most of all, he gives me love.
My dad, my friend.

Habibur Rahman (10)

Favourite Friend

Fabulous, fiery, funny friend,
Artistic, amazing, acrobatic friend,
Vivacious, vibrant, vatic friend,
Optimistic, outgoing, outstanding friend,
Radiant, restless, responsible friend,
Interesting, incredible, irreplaceable friend,
Troublesome, terrific, talented friend,
Excitable, energetic, exotic friend.

Fantastic, friendly, flexible friend,
Revolutionary, random, rocking friend,
Imaginative, inspirational, intelligent friend,
Entertaining, educated, elegant friend,
Nice, natural, nutty friend,
Dreamy, devoted, dotty friend.

That's my favourite friend!

Zoe Laxton (10)

My Grandad, Paul

My grandad, Paul, is someone to have a ball with.
His poems and stories I adore,
But annoy the people next door.
Mr Murphy is his mate,
He comes through the garden gate,
Making Grandad's garden look really great.
Me and Grandad have secret snacks,
We always cover each other's back.
Grandad sometimes sings along
To his favourite country songs.
He used to read me nursery rhymes,
But now he reads the Sunday Times.
Grandad is so special to me,
Without him it wouldn't be
The Field family.

Ceri-Ann Field (10)

I Am Lucky . . .

I am lucky . . .
To have a brother
Who is like no other

He is sometimes funny
And loves money

He is like no other
That's my brother

Even when times get rough
He always stays tough

He never fails to amaze
Now hear this phrase
My brother . . .
He will take any quest
And is better than the rest!

Zainab Patel (11)

My Best Friend

I have a dog called Red,
He is my furry friend,
When he was a pup
He would love to jump up
And roll around on the ground
Like an army man.

He likes to rip up his bed,
But I give him his bone instead.
He always will adore
Going to explore,
He likes to have fun
And loves to run.

Sometimes he drives me round the bend,
But even then he's still my best friend.

Isaac Lowry (10)

Favourite Teacher

He stood before the dirtied whiteboard,
His words soft but convincing,
Making the tedious topic of beaches
Come to life.

My favourite teacher
Stood there sculpting
Piles of shingle out of words,
Beaches scattered with pebbles.

My favourite teacher
Stood there juggling numbers,
Twisting problems and multiplying numbers,
Making them leap off the whiteboard
And perform acrobatics
Before jumping into our heads.

Eliza Wren (10)

My Wonderful Aunty Glenda

I can't believe you have gone
You were brilliant, you were strong
You were lovely, you were kind
You were always on my mind
You were the best by far
And now you are a beautiful star.

I loved it when you held me tight
I wanted to stay there all through the night
But unfortunately I had to go
I *really* didn't want to though!

It seems like you are far, far away
But you are probably with me this very day.

Anna Fitzgeorge (11)

My Mum

One of my favourite people is my mum,
Yet I'm eleven years old.
She still tucks me in at night
And even does when I'm very bold!

We always go places
That my three brothers don't,
And I always get things
That my brothers specially want.

And most of all I love my mum
And she loves me,
And we're both very happy
With our family.

Beth Conroy (11)

Friends

Some friends are good
Some friends are bad
Some are just happy
Some are very sad

Some friends yelp
Some friends scream
Some friends are crazy
Some are not what they seem

Some friends are helpful
Some friends are nice
Some friends are chatty
Most friends think twice.

Olivia Brewin (8)

My Favourite Person

My cat is quite unique
When he struts his stuff down our street.
He's sleek and black with silent paws
And he's so gentle with his claws.

He snuggles up to me in bed,
A good replacement for my ted.
He whispers softly in my ear,
Whiskery purrs to show he's near.

When I go to school he looks fantastic,
Snugly curled up in his basket.
Toulouse, the cat, is my best friend,
He'll be my favourite until the end.

Eve Patton (9)

My Dog Nico

My dog is Nico
He is a boy
He sometimes jumps
Or plays with his toy.

When he's bored
He likes to bark
Which tells me
It's time for the park.

First he walks
Then he'll run
It's very tiring
But lots of fun.

Kurran Landa (10)

Alice

My favourite person's Alice
The best a friend could be
Even when she's far away
She's always there for me.

I couldn't find a better friend
Even if I searched the Earth
She's my best friend, no one else's
No one else knows what she's worth.

She lives so very far away
Yet even when she isn't near
She's always very close to me
In my heart she's always here.

Willa Elliot (11)

I Love My Mummy!

I love my mummy
Because she is as fun as can be
And when I'm sad she makes me really happy
That's why I love my mummy.

My mummy's the best
Because she cooks really yummy food
And puts me in a good mood
That's why my mummy's the best.

My mummy's the greatest
Because she is kind and caring
And always is sharing
That's why my mummy's the greatest.

Melanie Gunetilleke (11)

My Favourite Person

My hero has fun in pairs,
Never found lazing in chairs.
A great explorer and finder too
Used to be known as; say who?

Time-traveller extraordinaire
Spiky, funky, gelled-brown hair
A clever man and far from bald
He is good-looking and very, very old.

Usually wears clean socks,
Travels in a spinning blue box.
Exciting, intelligent and always new,
He's a hundred and two, it's Doctor Who.

Amy Phillips (9)

Mum

My favourite person is, in fact, my mum,
Who cares when you cry and gets a job well done!

Mothers sometimes tell you off
And tell you to do things you don't want to do.
You then think they don't love you,
When in actual fact they do!
They'll guide you through your life,
Through thick and thin,
And even though they pretend to tease
They won't ever actually throw you in the bin!

So trust and care for your mum with all your heart,
And know from this day on you shall never part!

Kristin Russell-Rickards (10)

Fletcher

Fletcher is my neighbour's dog,
I treat him like my own.
He wags his tail when he sees me,
But I have to remember he's on loan.

I love Fletcher very much,
We have a special bond.
Every time we go to the park,
He always jumps in the pond.

Fletcher is seven years old
But still as playful as a puppy,
And when he sees a tennis ball,
He's very jumpy-uppy!

Jemma Watson (11)

My Dog Jess

My dog, Jess, is a really cute puppy
She plays with me and gets really mucky

She's a golden retriever
Who gets upset whenever I leave her

We practise tricks every day
Then after that we go and play

It would break my heart
If we were to part
Because we have been together
From the start.

I love you Jess!

Olivia Alexander (10)

The Person That I Like

The person that I like is called Fiona Denvir
I think her birthday is on the first of September
It slipped my mind a few weeks ago
So just listen about my friend and let the poem flow
I met her on the first day of school
And I like her because she's really cool
I think Fiona is smart and is someone I can trust
I am writing this because I like her and I must
Me and Fiona like to sing and dance
So if we get the time we have a little prance
Me and Fiona's likings are practically the same
Oh, I nearly forgot, James is my name.

James Stuart Rennie (10)

Me, My Dad And My Motorbike

Me and my dad
Zoom up the road
Me and my dad
Skid down the hill
Me and my dad
Race across a field
Me and my dad
Jump over a river
Me and my dad
Wheelspin in mud
Me and my dad
Speed up a ramp.

Jack Rossiter (10)

Tommy, My Favourite Person

My favourite person isn't really a person,
It's a thing.
My favourite thing isn't really a thing,
It's an animal,
An animal who's very talented
In his own special way,
But it's sad to say that he isn't be with us anymore,
So you won't get to see his talent, not now, not any day.
Tommy was everything to me,
My best friend, my pet.
I can still remember, he's still clear in my mind.
I suppose he was and still is, caught up in my friendship net.

Phoebe Collingridge (11)

Untitled

My name is Kareena,
I'm five years old.
It go to school full-time.
My favourite person is my dad,
He gives me everything I want.
I love all food,
But my favourite is pasta bake.
My mum makes the best.
My best friend is Bronte,
She is so cool.
I love going to school
And playing all day long.

Kareena Akhtar (5)

My Mum

My mum is funny and sweet,
The one person you'd love to meet.
She's pretty and small,
Not like me at all.
She can lose her temper,
But her bark's worse than her bite.
My mum is my role model,
I love her so much!
She comforts me when I'm hurt.
My mum is my favourite person
In the whole wide world.
Mum, I love you ever so much.

Zara Nicol (11)

My Favourite Person

Fast asleep I lie until a soft voice gently awakens me.
'Wake up, it's time for school.'
She plaits my hair,
She cooks me breakfast,
She plays with me,
As well as making my birthdays special
She encourages me in life
And helps me in tricky situations.
She stands by me,
She sticks with me
And I'm proud to say . . .
Lydia's my sister and I love her to bits.

Adele Harris (11)

My Mum

She's bossy, she's clumsy,
She might make me cry,
But inside I know she loves to make me smile!
She's got big brown eyes and a cheeky grin,
But sometimes she gets me in a spin.
She takes me everywhere,
Even when she's broke.
One time, she even took me to Stoke!
It doesn't matter where we are,
Together we are two shining stars!
My mum, she's great,
She's my best mate!

Zanjeeb Butt (10)

To My Grandmother

I remember crawling into your hands and you gently picked me up.
I looked into your big, brown eyes and I wrapped my hand around your finger
As I grew up I watched the difference you've made in lives of others.
You have become fragile and weak but I know deep down in my heart
                                                                you are still strong.
Suddenly I watched you go to hospital my heart was broken
                                                                 into tiny, little fragments.
After one helpless year without you, you finally came out.
I grew up some more watching you make a difference to the world.
And having a happy life but don't you ever forget I love you with all my heart.
You are the person that completes my life.
That's why you are my favourite person in the world!

Diveena Nanthakumaran (11)

My Mum's The Best

Dear Diary
My mum's so full of wisdom and love
No wonder God sent her down from above
My mum is like a flower
No wonder she's so sweet
I can see that gleam in her eyes
But like a crystal there is a surprise
My mum is the best
She helps me in my test
My sister's in a number one school
So I think my mum's the best part
No wonder I am so smart.

Promise Emesi (9)

My Lady

She comforts me when I am sad,
Doesn't tell me off when I'm bad.
She wakes me in the morning light
With a waggy tail and eyes so bright.
She runs in the garden, full of grace,
A happy look all over her face.
She stays with me all night and day
And hates it if I go away.
But most of all she's my best friend,
Not a toy and not a trend,
Because my dog, Lady, she loves me,
And she means all the world to me!

Georgina McCann (10)

My Dad

My dad
Like a superhero from above
He covers me with his kindness and love
Truly honest and always smiles
Like a friend that lasts for whiles
He knows what to say
Even on the darkest days
He never fails to cheer me up
Like a cup of fizzy pop
This is my favourite person in the whole of 2009
Because he's like my Superman
And I'm his super fan.

Victor Salako (11)

My Little Brother

My brother is so funny
He has a little bunny
He's not very tall
But thinks he's Mr Know-It-All
He has a lot of toys
That he uses to make noise
He crashes them and bashes them
And has a lot of fun with them
I try to get him to be quiet
But then it turns into a crazy riot
It's not much fun
But now it's over with and done.

Sarrah Boukheroufa (9)

Sophie Coates Is Not Only My Sister By My Best Friend

We'd lie for each other,
Probably even die for each other,
We have our downs and frowns, but hey, who doesn't?
We just seem to wipe our sad tears away,
And start to make each other's day!
When we see each other our eyes light up as bright as ever!
I can't explain how close we are,
Let's just say like two peas in a pod
You may think it's all a bunch of jokes,
But I'm telling you folks it's all true!

Demi Coates (11)

Monty Panesar, My Favourite Person

West Indies start to fear
Australia if you dare
Summer's here, we are ready
England's ready.

Monty's on the crease
See the stumps fall
The long walk back
Another run, another ball.

Straight and true, I admire you
To watch you bowl
That's my goal.

Kiran Banerjee (8)

Friendships Worth More Than Fame

I like Zac Efron, Madonna and cheeky Alesha too
But Imogen's my favourite person
She tops them all, it's true

When I see her I run to her, fast as a cat to a mouse
With arms wide open and a gleaming smile
That says you're my favourite person
Yes, definitely you

Best friends are important
It's definitely true
So when you see your best friend
Tell them what they mean to you.

Rachel Ann Marsh (9)

My Little Cousin

My little cousin toddles round the place,
Without a care in the world,
Like she's in a race.

My little cousin on her rocking horse,
Up and down,
Up and down,
She's like a mini clown.

My little cousin,
I really love her a lot,
But because she's only one,
She still sleeps in a cot.

Melissa Fear (9)

When He Leaves I Wonder

I have a friend called Timy
He's a furry friend you know
But I just can't help but wonder
What happens when he goes.

Is he a cool cat with lots of friends and fans?
Or is he a clumsy clogs who always needs a hand?
I know, he's a disco cat who dances all night long
Or maybe he's a singer cat who likes to sing a song.

It's funny if he is these things
All he does at home is eat and sleep
And lie about then leaves and I'm alone.

Lily-Rose Morris-Zumin (9)

Grandads Are Great

All grandads are great, especially mine
He is the best, I remember the good times
He's the one I look up to
And I remember when he fixed my bike too
I will love him more and more
He's the one that shared his biscuits from the cupboard door
He cuddled me when I was hurt
Loved all the good times that we shared
I will look up to him
Even though I ate his biscuits when he wasn't home
All the times, all the fun, I love him to the bone.

Samuel Portwood (11)

My Favourite Person, Lauren

Imagine having a friend like Lauren,
Seeing her will always make me smile.
Me and Lauren stick together,
Not tomorrow or the other, forever.
Imagine having a friend like Lauren,
Supportive and kind all the time.
She is so funny, got hair like a bunny.
Imagine having a friend like Lauren,
We have sleepovers at night,
We get snacks and never frighten the cat.
I just imagine you have a friend like Lauren too.

Freya Seekings (10)

Leanne

My friend Leanne is so cool
Even though she's tough,
She totally rules!
She's wicked at football
And cricket of course.
I still wonder why her
Favourite animal is not a horse
She has a brother who is totally quiet.
Did I mention he is such a riot.
So I have come to the end of my spontaneous poem
Now it's time for me to get going.

Naomi Nioku (10)

Liberty

My favourite person has to be
My best friend, Liberty.
She's always there when I feel sad
And even though I'm slightly mad
She likes me as I am, I'm glad.
We've been together for so long
And now our friendship has become strong.
She makes me laugh, she makes me cry,
She makes me wet my pants sometimes!
And now you can see this is why
Liberty's that mad friend of mine.

Louisa Sanderson (11)

My Best Friend

My favourite person is my best friend
She is awesome
It's fun to play lots of games with her
If you say coming out to play?
You'll have a great time
If you fall she's there to help
You never feel left out
Do you wanna play ball?
She will usually call
If you're left out
That's my best friend and this is the end.

Caitlin Collins (10)

My Sister Lilly-Ann

My little sister is the best
I love her so much
Even more than Mum
She's pretty
She's beautiful
I hug her and feed her
And pat her back
I hold her hands in the bath
So she doesn't feel scared
But when she cries I give her back to my mum
I still love my little sister, she's the best.

Benjamin Juliff (5)

My Best Friends

Every time I see them
It fills me with joy
And all my worries go away.

We love to play,
I wish they would never go,
But I have to say goodbye.

Now I don't see them very much
As they are very far away,
But every time the sun shines
I know they're around to play.

Chloe May (11)

Anthony Horowitz

You cannot beat a brilliant book
With a great and intriguing hook
I know who can provide just the thing
With a tense action style of novel writing.

He also does some screenplay and loads of other stuff
But of his thrilling novels, I just can't get enough
Oh how I would love to have a job like his
Adventures and horror are his specialities.

But I'd have trouble matching wits
With the one and only Anthony Horowitz.

Marco Cardoni (11)

My Favourite Cousin

My favourite person is someone very special
She really is one of a kind
My favourite person is someone very close to my heart
She really is the best you will ever find.

My favourite person is my favourite of all
My cousin Laura is there when I fall
Whenever I need her, she is there
Someone to laugh with, I know that she really cares.

No matter what happens, she will always be
The best ever cousin *in history!*

Kirsty Brickles (11)

Alien!

My brother is an alien
He lives inside my mum
He's growing, expanding and pushing out her tum!

He has a large head
His hands are very small
I'm not sure he can hear me
He has no ears at all!

Although some may say he's rather grim
But I love him
He is my favourite little thing.

Millie Lépora (11)

My Brother, Sean

My brother, Sean, drives me up the wall,
Round the bend and makes me loopy
With some of the things he's said and done,
But I know he loves me the most.
I would feel embarrassed to boast
Just how great my brother, Sean, is.
When I'm down he is always around
With a tissue, a hug or 100% of love.
That's why my brother, Sean, is the best
And wears his badge with pride.

Rachel Cullen (12)

This One Goes To . . .

When I see a smile
Getting up is worth my while
This one goes to all my friends
The fun and jokes will never end.

Megan Campbell (12)

My Mate Reece!

This boy I know Reece D'Abreu, plays with me at half-past two
We play all night, we play all day
I miss Reece when I go away
There's lots of things I like to do with this boy called Reece D'Abreu
We both like the characters from the Yu-Gi-Oh show
Pokémon and Digimon, anything goes
I support Man U, he's an Arsenal fan
Devils and Gunners together, tackle anything we can
Our skin is different, but no matter it holds
Because our friendship is stronger and better than gold.

Macauley Hatley (10)

Konie!

Konie is a special girl
She is always delightful,
Her eyes shine, she's got long curly hair
Konie always gives me a stare,
She counts her pennies one by one
She looks at me and realises they are gone,
She is disabled, she always smiles
It doesn't stop her travelling miles,
But to me she's an ordinary girl,
But to all of us she's a very special girl.

Callum Burkitt (10)

Eleanor - Haiku

I picked Eleanor
Eleanor is my best friend
And she always smiles.

Ellie Bannister (10)

Mum

I love my mum,
She's a star in the sky,
She takes me where I wish to go
And soothes me if I stub my toe.
She's loving and sweet, with a heart of gold,
So I always do what I've been told.
So when I'm being good and sweet,
She rewards me with a yummy treat.
And that's the lady I adore,
So really I can't ask for more.

Callum Draycott (11)

My Dad

My dad is ginger, he thinks he's a ninja
Football is his game, he says he feels no pain
He's a bog-hogging dad,
He sits on the pot and sings a lot.
My dad is strong, he's like King Kong
He's very hairy but he's as light as a fairy.
My dad will always love me.
I know this much is true,
So when he tucks me in at night
I tell him I love him too!

Francesca Leftley (11)

My Best Friend

My best friend, she is the best
We have fun in school in maths, English, history
You know the rest
She is always there when I am sad
She sticks by me side through good and bad
She has been my best friend for almost three years
I think this calls for a celebration
'Everyone, three cheers.'
She has been moody, she has been a pain
But she is my best friend called Chloe-Jayne.

Amy Davies (11)

My Mum

My mum is special
Because she saved my life
When I had a gobstopper
Stuck in my throat.
I was turning blue.
My mum whacked my back
And I yacked,
After that it came out
With a shot.
I thought I'd had my lot!

Emily Owen (9)

My Mother

My mother is the light at the end of my tunnel
The sun in my sky
And the sweet sounds in my ears.

My mother is the colour in my life
The idol in my eyes
And the elegant petal on my flower.

My mother is my greatest friend
She is always there for me through thick and thin
That is why my mother is my favourite person!

Emily Lee (11)

My Favourite Person!

He loves to cook,
He buys me books,
Unfortunately he is not blessed with looks.

He makes me smile,
We walk for miles,
Continually talking all the while.

He belongs to Mum,
But now the time has come
For me to say I love him.

Alicia Clarke (9)

Daddy Cool!

My favourite person is crazy and fun
He likes a good sticky bun
Whilst sitting in the sun!

He loves watching football of his favourite team
Eating cheesy Doritos
And a bit of ice cream!

He is a great painter and loves the colour blue
He also loves drawing
Especially pictures of my favourite cartoon.

Ebonie Barnes (11)

My Favourite Person 2009

My favourite person is my mother.
Her name is Dorothy Oforiwaa,
She was born on 13th August 1975.
She is tall, light in complexion.
She is my favourite person because she is my mentor.
She is god-fearing and a lovely person.
She likes me a lot and teaches me
A lot of good things, like how to cook
And how to take good care of myself.

Kelly Oforiwaa (6)

Robyn

She is always there for you,
Special, kind and funny,
Like a warm teddy bear,
As precious as a flower,
She makes you feel cosy.
Robyn.
She makes me feel
As important as the Queen.
She will be there forever.

Holly Gooding (11)

The Best Mum In The World

Roses are red, violets are blue
Mum I love you
You are lovely and kind, beautiful too
You're the best mum in the world, thank you
Kind and caring, even when we are down
You help us to understand things
No one else could make us understand, so thank you
You're my favourite person in the whole wide world
I just wanted you to know that I love you.

Billie Foster (10)

My Dad

My dad likes walking
My dad likes talking
My dad likes tea
My dad likes the sea
My dad likes nice food
It puts him in a good mood
But altogether my dad likes me!

Lucy Osborne (9)

My Little Cousin

Trey is my little cousin,
He was born eight weeks ago.
He likes to drink his bottle
Which helps to make him grow.
He likes to laugh and wiggle.
I hide my face to jump out and say, 'Boo!'
He is a happy baby but sometimes he cries,
I think he needs his nappy changed,
Now that's not a surprise!

Emily Gibbs (10)

Sky (My Cat)

Sky is a soft furry cushion perched on a chair
Sky is a tiny lizard running for cover
Sky is a posh lady nibbling at her meat
Sky is a ravenous lion scoffing her biscuits
Sky is a noisy cockerel waking me up in the morning
Sky is a sneaky snake seeking a cosy place to sleep
Sky is a rolling ball of happiness
Sky is a fluffy bundle of fur chasing me round the garden
Sky is a precious gem that I love to bits.

Amy Lewington (10)

My Mum

Shopping for clothes and handbags
In John Lewis and Louis Vuitton
Sitting in the sun with her new clothes on
Eating out at restaurants with coffee and some chocs
Beside her sits Paul in a bright pair of socks
She is my favourite person, of course
Let's just give her a round of applause.

Daniel Davies (10)

My Favourite Person

This person makes me laugh
And shouts, 'Get in that bath!'
She has a laugh like Muttley, the cartoon dog,
And she certainly isn't keen on eggnog.
She loves to sing and dance
And always makes a grand entrance.
She knows quite a lot about glamour,
So as people of New England say,
I love my gramma.

Sophie Lancelot (11)

Last Day At Infants

In the morning when I wake,
The sun shone through the daybreak.
While my books were in my bag,
I'd make my way to school so glad.
Miss Moss you taught me well,
Even taught me how to spell.
In the year I spent with you,
My day was never ever blue.
That's why I miss you.

Grace Benfield (9)

My Uncle Arnie Is My Favourite Person

A rnie is the best uncle in the world!
R ules like a cool dude, I like his style and looks
N ice, kind and always funny, always great to see him!
I love Arnie, he plays with me and tells me jokes,
                             he makes me laugh!
E very day when I think of him, he makes me smile
                  because he's my favourite person.

Jade Mall (9)

Special Mum

My mum is my favourite person
She is the best
She keeps me clean and warm and fed
She tucks me up all snug in bed
And tells me to rest my tired head
She'll tell me off if I get into trouble
And help me out if I get in a muddle
I love my mum, she is the best
Better than all the rest.

Aisha Dechicha (6)

My Mum

My mum is my best friend.
She looks after me
And the whole family.

She makes me smile,
Not just once in a while,
All the time.

I'm really lucky to have a mum like her,
So that's why my mum is my best friend.

Natasha Richardson (10)

My Favourite Person

My favourite person is Jessica Brody Benis
We are classmates and she is hardworking
With school work and activities
She is cute, lovely, friendly and very accommodating
She puts a smile on my face and is one out of a million
She is that light that glitters in my dark moments
She is that sunshine everyone would like to have.

Jennifer Shawulu Nggada (6)

My Favourite Person

My favourite person is my brother
But sometimes I wish I had another!
He can be quite a pain,
The date of our birthday is the same.
He likes to use tools
And swim in swimming pools.
These are our names,
Eleanor and James!

Eleanor Lowe (9)

My Bunny, Max

Here are some facts
About my bunny, Max.
He's like a meerkat
When he stands on his two back feet.
When he lifts up his long, pointy ears,
He can hear a mouse squeak.
Do I really have to go to school today?
Because I could cuddle him all day!

Joanna Sands (9)

My Legendary Grandads!

My legendary grandads
How they are just the best
They mean the world to me
And they're better than the rest
They are my shining superstars
They stand out from the crowd
I give them all the love I've got
And I'm so very proud!

Erin Lawlor (11)

Dad

Dad I Love You
Dad you are so glad
Dad I love you
Sometimes you go on holiday or I do
I still will remember you
I am here for you
Wherever you go
I will always love you.

Jazmin Lake (9)

My Mum

My mum's the best
She cares for me
She always make me
Smile and be happy
And when I am sad
And all alone
She picks me up
And takes me home.

Katelyn Reeves (9)

Adebayor

A debayor is cool
D riving in a Ferrari
E very single day
B anging in the goals
A gainst every team
Y o-yo Adebayor
O h Adebayor
R un, run Adebayor.

Robert Warden (10)

Billie And Millie

I have a dog called Millie
And she acts really silly.
She has a brother Billie
And they play really, really silly.
Sometimes Millie gets prickly
And Billie gets tickly
And they make me giggly.
I love them both so much.

Rhiannon Thomas (6)

My Grandma

My grandma is my best friend
We have fun playing pretend
She may be old but my best friend
Knows how to be there in the end
If I am sad she loves me
If I am bad she scolds me
But my best friend is my grandma,
She is always there for me.

Connor Knill (11)

My Favourite Person

My best friend is kind.
My best friend is mine.
My best friend is caring.
But also very daring.
My best friend is funny.
And also bright and sunny.
My best friend is there for me every single day.
We love and care for each other in every single way.

Lucy Geoghegan (11)

My Mum

My mum's feeling down
But I won't let her drown.
I'll pick her back up,
Get her out of the muck.
If she cries and cries,
I'll dry both her eyes,
My mum is my favourite person ever,
I will never leave her ever.

Olivia Sims (10)

My Favourite Person

Farhana is cool, Farhana is fun,
I think she is number one.
Farhana is cool, Farhana is the best,
I think she never takes a rest.
My aunt Farhana, is the best,
She is funny, silly and sometimes a pest.
We play, laugh and fight,
She takes me to the park and we play with the kite.

Inthesar Ar-Rahman (9)

Johnny Depp

The crowd are silent,
Getting their cameras ready,
Just waiting.
Later on a limo pulls up,
Noise rises from the crowd.
A fairly tall man steps out
With two bodyguards surrounding him.
The crowd follow him wherever he goes.

Ethan Good (10)

My Nan

My nan
To me is the best
She looks after me when I need a helping hand
To me that is a great nan
She is there whatever the need is
I love her and she loves me
And that's all I care about
She's the greatest person in the land!

Chloe Human (10)

My Best Friend

My best friend is Kyle.
Kyle is very agile,
He likes Doctor Who
And purple shoes,
He *loves* cheese,
But *hates* Jason Vorhees.
Kyle will be my best friend
Right through till the very end.

Hamish Wilson (11)

Mum And Dad

I really can't decide which parent is my favourite
So I picked them both and would like to share it
Mum is always caring and her rules are almost none
Dad understands when I'm feeling blue and is lots of fun
Mum always hugs me when I'm sad
Dad has good tips when my cuts are bad
I really can't decide and I hope you don't mind
My parents both are brilliant, they are one of a kind!

Lauren Ivy Walsh (9)

My Granda

My granda who's funny, artistic and fun
Is loving and caring but all around fun
I know everyone else's grandas are fine
But no one has such as mine
He picks me up from school in his big new car
And drops me home which isn't far
He says I look nice in my new school dress
He always calls me his little princess.

Orlagh McCloskey (10)

Ronaldo

R uns rings round Veira
O n his head it goes
N ow it's flying into the net
A mazing Ronaldo scores again
L ooks at Rooney with a wink
D arts around to lift the cup
O h no, he's leaving the club.

Lewis Kettlety (8)

My Little Furry Friend

My favourite person isn't a person at all
He's only 12 inches tall
He comforts me when I'm mad
And makes me happy when I'm sad
Soft and furry, he lies between me and the wall
But me and my furry friend
Will never play football.

Michael Wales (8)

The Best Person, Tallulah

Short hair, blonde hair,
Short and skinny.
She's snazzy,
She's funny and
She's my best friend.
I like her, I do,
Until the end.

Miranda Tossell Laszkiewicz (9)

My Sister

I sometimes call my sister a blister,
But really I love her dearly.
There is no one like my sister, Bethany,
She is a magnificent little three-year-old.
Without her I would be lonely and sad.
My sister, Bethany, is my favourite person,
And those are the reasons why, plus - she isn't bad.

Bryony Gooch (10)

Funny Friends

My friend is always laughing at everything I say,
We're the best of friends in every single way.
We both like exploring, we love animals too,
But not scooping up their poo!
We're very daring, the two of us.
We're really good at tennis,
But we don't like Denis the Menace.

Hollie Symmons (8)

My Favourite Person

My sister is really nice,
Although we always tend to fight.
We like to play together all the time,
Even though she takes things that are mine.
But at the end of the day,
She is my sister and she knows
That I love her more than ever.

Courtney Lewis (10)

My Dog

O ld and dopey, he walks into the garden.
L etting no one disturb him.
I n his low-toned voice he barks and rumbles.
V ets are his worst nightmare.
E ating his slimy dinner with a slurp.
R esting in his cosy, warm bed.
    My dog Oliver!

Lucy Knight-Summers (11)

Untitled

My favourite person is my best friend Connor
Because he is a good singer
He makes me laugh
We like to play on the Xbox 360 together
We always have fun
I like to go to his house for tea
We have pizza and chips with tomato sauce.

Ryan Munro (8)

My Friend Ashley

A wesome Ashley
S illy Ashley
H appy Ashley
L oving Ashley
E veryone likes her
Y ou're my best friend.

Beth Alice Edmonds (11)

My Favourite Person

I went with my dad and we bought a hamster,
It is furry and brown and goes round and round,
It sleeps in the morning and wakes me at night,
She seems very nice and very friendly too,
Her name is Ruby and mine is not,
She's my favourite pet and I'm her favourite person.

Fatima Noor (10)

Emily

My furry friend lives around the bend.
Across the street is where we meet.
She is a cat that sleeps on my mat.
She is very kind and tabby-lined.
She is sensitive and furry
And as sweet as a cherry.

Caitlin McMullan (9)

Untitled

My favourite person is filled with glee
My favourite person is like Superman
I like cars and so does he
My brother who I can't live without
My amigo, my friend, but most importantly
My brother.

Brandon Carter (10)

My Dad

My favourite person is my dad,
He is the best one I've ever had.
He cheers me up when I am sad,
Sometimes he gets a little mad.
Not even once has he been bad,
He is always a jolly good lad.

Lewis Isaac (9)

Favourite Person

My favourite person is the best friend in the world,
She's so kind and funny and always there for me.
Her eyes sparkle in the sun,
Her hair blows in the wind like a princess.
She is the princess in my life,
My friend, Kimi.

Jessica Tennant (11)

My Black Lab Benson

B est boy
E ver! However
N aughty he can be but
S o, because I love him
O ver the moon and back again
N o other dog could be as great as my black Lab.

Maddie Hardern (9)

My Family

My favourite person is . . .
Mum is special, Mum is great
Dad is funny, my best mate
Joe is a pain, but I love him really
And Daisy my rabbit just sleeps and eats daily
That's my family and they are all my favourite.

Chloe Pitman (10)

My Mum And Dad

My mum's hair is so nice,
It looks like a daisy.
My dad is very tall.
Mum and Dad love me very much
And I love my mum and dad
Very much too.

Daniel Lock (9)

My Purr-fect Person

My favourite person is warm and fluffy like a hot-water bottle
She snuggles next to me when I am heavy-hearted
Her delectable purr is soothing as an angel's song.
Her fur brightens when in the sun
When she is asleep she is heavenly
My favourite person is my wonderful, adorable cat named Maddie.

Jodie Passmore (11)

My Grandad

This poem's for my grandad,
He always makes me smile.
I've never seen him sad,
His face beaming for a mile.
Days with him go so quick,
Burning like a candlewick.

Sarah Edwards (11)

My God

He might not be a person,
He might not be real
But to me He's everything.
Many people call Him the real deal.
He might not be beside me,
He might not be there at all,
But what I do know is that He's Lord, Lord of all.
He might not live in a house,
He might not live in a mansion,
But His address is churches,
Churches around the world and its oceans.
He might be really transparent,
He might be invisible,
But to me He's glorious and invincible.
He might not be a postman,
He might not drive a bus,
But His job is to take care of all of us.
He might not be a rock star,
He might not be a cook
But He's very famous in writing the bible, His book.
He might not be smart,
He might not be the cleverest in the world,
But do remember that He made us, boys and girls.
I might not know everyone,
I might not know about you,
But God is my favourite person,
Why don't you make Him yours too?

Godgift Emesi (11)

My Favourite Person - A Shining Star

Young Writers Information

We hope you have enjoyed reading this book - and that you will continue to enjoy it in the coming years.

If you like reading and writing poetry drop us a line, or give us a call, and we'll send you a free information pack.

Alternatively if you would like to order further copies of this book or any of our other titles, then please give us a call or log onto our website at www.youngwriters.co.uk

Young Writers Information
Remus House
Coltsfoot Drive
Peterborough
PE2 9JX
(01733) 890066